2004

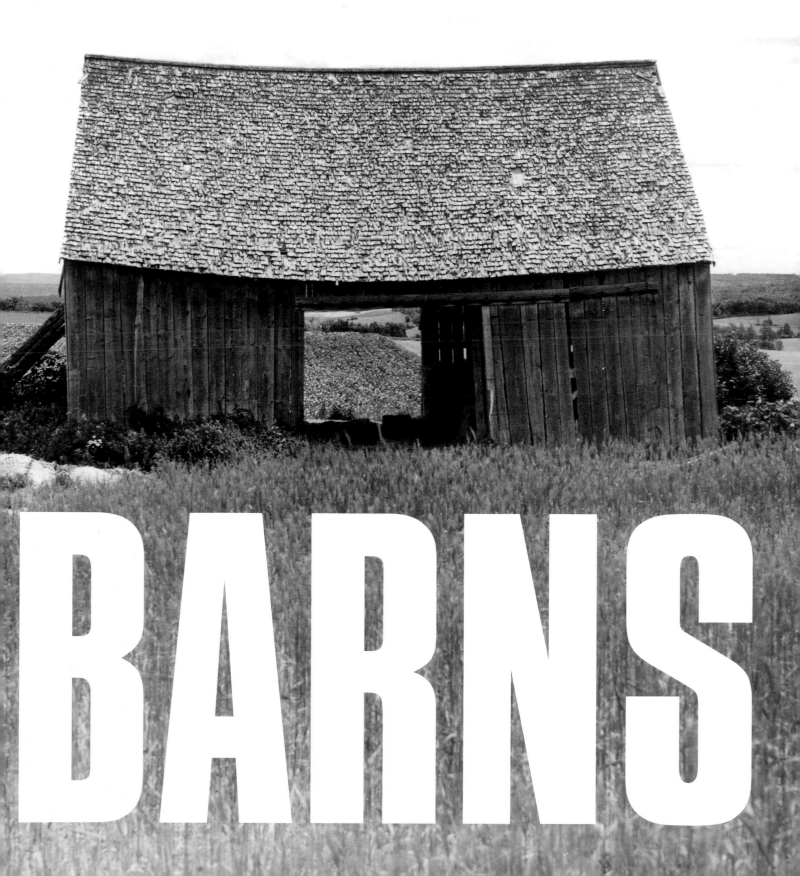

BARNS

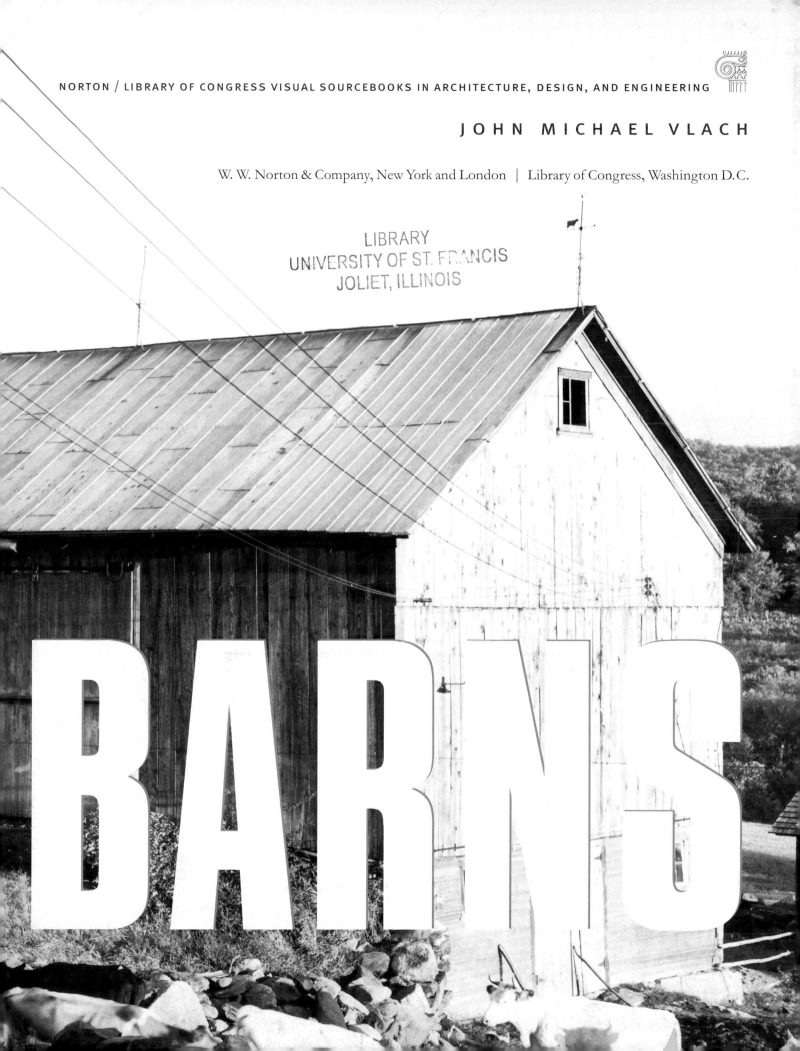

NORTON / LIBRARY OF CONGRESS VISUAL SOURCEBOOKS IN ARCHITECTURE, DESIGN, AND ENGINEERING

JOHN MICHAEL VLACH

W. W. Norton & Company, New York and London | Library of Congress, Washington D.C.

BARNS

FOR ARCHIE GREEN

Master builder, masterful scholar

Copyright © 2003 by Library of Congress
Copyright © 2003 by John Michael Vlach

For information about permission to reproduce
selections from this book, write to Permissions,
W. W. Norton & Company, Inc., 500 Fifth Avenue,
New York, NY 10110

Manufacturing by Courier-Westford
Book Design by Kristina Kachele
Production Manager: Leeann Graham

*Norton/Library of Congress Visual Sourcebooks
in Architecture, Design, and Engineering*
Editorial Board
Robert Bruegmann
David G. De Long
Nancy N. Green
C. Ford Peatross

Library of Congress
Cataloging-in-Publication Data
Vlach, John Michael, 1948-
Barns / John Michael Vlach.
p. cm. — (Norton/Library of Congress
visual sourcebooks in architecture, design,
and engineering)
"Project of the Center for Architecture, Design
and Engineering in the Library of Congress"
—T.p.verso.
Includes bibliographical references and index.
ISBN 0-393-73086-7
1. Barns — United States. I. Center for
Architecture, Design and Engineering (U.S.)
II. Title. III. Series
NA8230 .V6 2003
728'.922'0973 — dc21   2002035741

W. W. Norton & Company, Inc.,
500 Fifth Avenue, New York, N.Y. 10110
www.wwnorton.com

W. W. Norton & Company Ltd.,
Castle House, 75/76 Wells St., London W1T 3QT

0 9 8 7 6 5 4 3 2 1

The Norton/Library of Congress Visual
Sourcebooks in Architecture, Design
and Engineering series is a project of the
Center for Architecture, Design and
Engineering in the Library of Congress,
established through a bequest from the
distinguished American architect Paul
Rudolph. The Center's mission is not
only to support the preservation of the
Library's enormously rich collections in
these subject areas, but also to increase the
public knowledge of and access to them.
Paul Rudolph hoped that others would
join him in supporting these efforts. The
Library of Congress is therefore pleased
to accept contributions to the Center for
Architecture, Design and Engineering
Fund or to the Paul Rudolph Trust to
further this progress, and to support
additional projects such as this one.

For further information on the Center
for American Architecture, Design and
Engineering, you may visit its website:
http://lcweb.loc.gov/rr/print/adecen-
ter/adecent.htm

The Center for Architecture, Design and Engineering and the Publishing Office of the Library of Congress are pleased to join with W. W. Norton & Company to inaugurate the pioneering series of the Norton / Library of Congress Visual Sourcebooks in Architecture, Design and Engineering.

Based on the unparalleled collections of the Library of Congress, this series of handsomely illustrated books is drawn from the collections of the nation's oldest federal cultural institution and the largest library in the world, with more than 120 million items on approximately 530 miles of bookshelves. The collections include more than 18 million books, 2.5 million recordings, 12 million photographs, 4.5 million maps, and 54 million manuscripts.

The subjects of architecture, design, and engineering are threaded throughout the rich fabric of this vast archive, and the books in this new series will serve not only to introduce researchers to the illustrations selected by their authors, but also to build pathways to adjacent and related materials, and even entire archives—to millions of photographs, drawings, prints, views, maps, rare publications, and written information in the general and special collections of the Library of Congress, much of it unavailable elsewhere.

Each volume will serve as an entry to the collections, providing a treasury of select visual material, much of it in the public domain, for students, scholars, teachers, researchers, historians of art, architecture, design, technology, and practicing architects, engineers, and designers of all kinds.

A CD-ROM accompanying each volume contains high-quality, downloadable, and uncropped versions of all the illustrations. It offers a direct link to the Library's online, searchable catalogs and image files, including the hundreds of thousands of high-resolution photographs, measured drawings, and data files in the Historic American Buildings Survey, Historic American Engineering Record, and, eventually, the recently inaugurated Historic American Landscape Survey. The Library's website has rapidly become one of the most popular and valuable locations on the internet, experiencing over three billion hits a year and serving audiences ranging from school children to the most advanced scholars throughout the world, with a potential usefulness that has only begun to be explored.

Among the subjects to be covered in this series are building types; building materials and details; historical periods and movements; landscape architecture and garden design; interior and ornamental design and furnishings; and industrial design. *Barns* is a superb exemplar of the possibilities and goals on which its series is based.

C. FORD PEATROSS

The introduction to this book provides a masterly overview of the development of a building type that has served to define the very nature and growth of the United States and its people. It is a view that is new and fresh and inspired by the depth and quality of the resources of the Library of Congress, and it substantially expands our knowledge of the subject. The balance of the book, containing 836 images, is organized into nine sections, by region. Figure-number prefixes designate the section. Note that letter designation following the figure number (for example, 1-034a) indicates that the image is a detail.

Short captions give the essential identifying information: subject, location, date, creator(s) of the image, and Library of Congress call number, which can be used to find the image online. Note that a link to the Library of Congress website may be found on the CD.

ABBREVIATIONS USED IN CAPTIONS

AM
American Memory

AFC
American Folklife Center

DPCC
Detroit Publishing Company Collection

FSA
Farm Security Administration

Gen. Coll.
General Collection

G & M
Geography and Map Division

HABS
Historic American Buildings Survey

HAER
Historic American Engineering Record

LC
Library of Congress

P & P
Prints and Photographs Division

CONTENTS

BARNS ACROSS AMERICA

THE BARN IN AMERICAN HISTORY

Writing in 1787 that "Those who labor in the earth are the chosen people of God," Thomas Jefferson promoted the virtues of a country devoted to agriculture hoping that the United States would one day become a nation of farmers.[1] As secretary of state, he was actually able to inscribe his plan onto the unsettled territories that lay beyond the Appalachian ranges when he championed the passage of the Land Ordinance of 1785. This set of regulations imposed a standardized survey system on the nation; the unsettled wilderness was apportioned into large square units called townships. Measuring six miles on a side, townships were divided further into thirty-six sections, each one a 640-acre parcel that was to be sold to an individual farmer.[2] The resulting national grid—a vast checkerboard of landholdings bounded by roads running north to south and east to west—was intended to encourage the swift expansion of agriculture across the continent. Given that the standard survey section was three to four times the size of the average farm, the lure of western land was very attractive. Jefferson's agrarian vision so inspired the fledgling nation that at the beginning of the nineteenth century close to 80 percent of all Americans lived on farms.[3] In such a country, farm buildings were clearly the most representative architectural expressions.

The new nation that Jefferson had imagined, an endless vista of fields and pastures interrupted only here and there by a village or two, became a reality. Benjamin Franklin confirmed the success of Jefferson's agrarian ideals when he observed that "The great business of the continent is agriculture. For one artisan, or merchant, I suppose that we have at least a hundred farmers."[4] In a nation of farmers, the long straight furrow, the

IN-001. N. Currier, *Smoking Him Out* (1848), New York, New York. P & P, LC-USZ62-40071.

SMOKING HIM OUT.

IN-001

tall haystack, the well-built house and barn were understood as the clearest signs of success and well-being. These were the visible proofs that a divinely chosen people had successfully undertaken the sacred mission to nurture the land and thus make of it a fruitful Eden.

But even as the farmer was becoming the emblematic American, the national will was beginning to focus on the competing promise of technological progress. Over the course of the nineteenth century success would no longer be marked exclusively by the size of the harvest but by the growth of cities, the rise of smoky factories, the building of railroads, and the invention of clever machines. The inventor and the mechanic (even the banker) would be lionized in a manner previously reserved for farmers. But the ascent of industry could not erase the image of the farmstead from the popular imagination. The sturdy plowman and his equally sturdy barn were deeply ingrained in American speech and custom. The barn, for example, became a standard point of reference for measure. Anything that was huge was usually said to be "as big as a barn." Anyone who made an errant throw was usually criticized as not being able "to hit the broad side of a barn." In 1848 barns even entered into the arena of politics when a group of northern politicians earned the nickname of "barn burners" for their zealous opposition to the expansion of slavery. The epithet originated in the story of a Dutch farmer who allegedly tried to solve a rat infestation by burning down his barn. A political cartoon of the day showed Martin Van Buren, who left the Democratic party to run on his

IN-002. Currier & Ives, *Home to Thanksgiving*, painted by John Schuller after a painting by George Henry Durie (1867) New York, New York. P & P, LC-USZ62-15.

IN-003. Currier & Ives, *Autumn in New England*, painted by John Schuller after a painting by George Henry Durie (1866), New York, New York. P & P, LC-USZ62-969.

IN-002

IN-003

own ticket, putting a torch to his barn while Democratic presidential candidate Lewis Cass jumps out of the roof, along with other rats (IN-001).

Throughout the middle decades of the nineteenth century the New York lithography company of Currier & Ives, which labeled itself "The Grand Central Depot for Cheap and Popular Pictures," produced numerous scenes for middle-class Americans to hang in their parlors. Often domestic in theme, the vast majority of their home scenes were depictions of rural settings.[5] These images portrayed the key elements of a farmstead, always including the house, the fields, and the barn. Even if the expressed theme was the four seasons, the cycle of life, or venerable holiday celebrations, the image of wholesome farm life was paramount (IN-002 and IN-003). Given that the audience for Currier & Ives was largely an urban one, these rural views functioned as nostalgic statements that encouraged an appreciation for a way of life quickly slipping into the past. By 1860 the United States had become so fully industrialized that the total value of the nation's manufactured goods was five times greater than all the crops raised by farmers.[6] By 1890 the American frontier was closed; there was no more open land to be settled. The nation

IN-004

IN-005

of farmers had transformed itself into a network of cities linked by an extensive system of railroads. By 1920 the majority of Americans lived in urban areas, and with so many Americans working in factories or close to urban areas, connections to country life faded into memories. Schoolchildren were routinely shown pictures of farms and barns to ensure that they would not forget where their food came from (IN-004).

The meteoric rise of an industrial economy did not, of course, signal the end of farming. While farmers were no longer viewed in venerable Jeffersonian terms, they surely remained proud of their achievements. During the last quarter of the nineteenth century farmers celebrated their efforts and their endurance in heroic views that appeared in hundreds of illustrated county atlases.[7] Most often produced for counties in the northeastern and midwestern states, these volumes were also assembled for sections of the Far West. Notifying farmers that an atlas of their county was about to be released, publishers offered to include pictures of their farms — for a fee. These images, especially those that were full-page vistas, presented farms in minute detail. A farmstead's house, fields, and barns are always shown along with its fences, windmills, haystacks, orchards, and livestock. Usually rendered from a bird's-eye perspective, the images made a farm seem like a vast, almost endless, holding. Meant to be flattering pieces of propaganda, farms were rendered as impossibly efficient and well-run estates where not so much as a blade of grass or a single leaf was out of place. Atlases show copious fields and promising orchards awaiting the harvest. The docile animals and fertile fields flatteringly marked each farmer as an American version of Adam in command of his own paradisiacal garden (IN-005–IN-008). Atlas artists gave their clients a visual claim to a level of social eminence that was, in fact, on the wane.

Barns, being the largest of farm buildings, were necessarily highlighted in these views. A barn might be the focus of a cameo vignette in the corner of a panoramic vista (IN-005) or the entire image could be arranged so that the barns and other sheds are shown in the foreground where they would stand out most forcefully (IN-007). Pride in one's

IN-004. Artist unknown, *The Farm Yard*, *Prang's Aids for Object Teaching* (1874), L. Prang and Co., Boston, Massachusetts. P & P, LC-USZ62-4434.

IN-005. Highland Farm, residence of John Armstrong, Brighton, Pennsylvania, *Illustrated Historical Centennial Atlas of Beaver County, Pennsylvania* (1876). P & P, LC-USZ62-31997.

IN-006

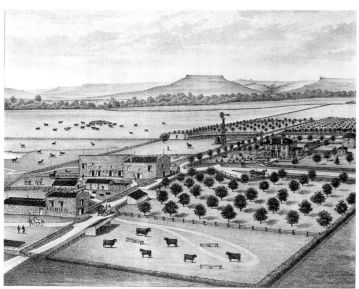

IN-007

IN-008

IN-006. Residence of J. C. Wilderman, St. Clair County, Illinois, Warner & Beers, *An Illustrated Historical Atlas of St. Clair County, Illinois* (1874). G & M, neg. no. 1312.

IN-007. Magnolia Farm, residence and stock farm of Arthur H. Greene, Edwards Brothers, *Illustrated Historical Atlas of Cowley County, Kansas* (1887). P & P, LC-USZ62-31972.

IN-008. Residence and farm of Mrs. R. Blagow, Alameda County, California, Thompson & West, *Official and Historical Atlas Map of Alameda County, California* (1878). G & M, neg. no. 885.

barn sometimes required that two views be commissioned, one that focused on the house and a second image that centered on the barn (IN-008).

When thinking about ways to embellish their farmsteads, farmers concentrated on their barns, making sure that they were not only sturdily built but attractive to the eye. This was especially true of barns from southeastern Pennsylvania, which were generally quite large and cleverly engineered (see 3-059–3-063). It was also common practice in the region to add brightly colored decorative designs to a barn (see 3-078). Often called "hex signs" in the tourist literature, the farmers said they were "barn stars" or "barn flowers."[8] These motifs, Germanic in origin, were used as well to embellish chairs, plates, powder horns, rifles, baptismal certificates, and gravestones. Their presence on the sides of barns served to connect these buildings into a full range of domestic expe-

IN-009

IN-010

IN-009. Hex signs and Holstein cow painted on a Pennsylvania barn. John Collier, photographer. P & P, LC-USF 34-082341-C.

IN-010. Design painted on a barn near Ephrata, Pennsylvania. John Collier, photographer. P & P, LC-USF 34-082342-C.

IN-011. Barn advertising in central Ohio. Ben Shahn, photographer. P & P, LC-USF 33-006477-M1.

I-011

riences as they declare, in a dramatic way, a farmer's ethnic or regional allegiances. Examples of Pennsylvania barn decoration from the middle decades of the twentieth century show an expansion of repertoire as images of livestock are combined with the older geometric motifs (IN-009 and IN-010). Such images announce a pride in production that was overtaking the need to proclaim one's ethnic roots. Beyond Pennsylvania the decoration of barns was confined mostly to portrayals of heroic animals (IN-011).[9]

A barn's immense size made it readily visible to any passersby. In the early years of the automotive age, advertisers crafted deals with farmers to use the walls of their barns as billboards. All manner of signs were painted but signs advertising Mail Pouch chewing tobacco were among the most common (IN-012–IN-014). Beginning around 1900

IN-013

IN-012

IN-012. Barn, Garret County, Maryland, being painted
with advertising signs. John Vachon, photographer.
P & P, LC-USF 34-060014-D.

IN-013. Barn with Mail Pouch Tobacco advertisement, Lancaster
County, Pennsylvania. Arthur Rothstein, photographer. P & P,
LC-USF 34-24505-D.

IN-014. Barn advertising, central Ohio. Ben Shahn, photographer.
P & P, LC-USF 33-006641-M3.

IN-015. Old barn in central Ohio. Ben Shahn,
photographer. P & P, LC-USF33-006564-M1.

IN-014

IN-015

teams of painters employed by the Bloch Brothers Tobacco Company were sent down numerous country lanes with orders to cover as many barns as possible with their slogan: "Chew Mail Pouch: Treat Yourself To The Best."[10] Harley Warwick of Belmont, Ohio, claimed to have painted over 20,000 such signs while ranging across much of the eastern United States over the course of a career that lasted more than fifty years. Very much a by-product of auto-tourism, these signs are now valued as the precious memorabilia of a bygone age.[11] They also signal a shift in the social understandings of the American barn. In the modern era when the family farm was fast becoming a vanishing institution, a barn—the farmer's most valued building—became little more than a place to post a bill (IN-015). Contemporary travelers along country roads are now more enthralled by the signs that they encounter than with the buildings on which they are painted.

THE HISTORY OF AMERICAN BARNS

The earliest American barns are best understood as immigrant gifts because they are all structures that can be traced back to a European homeland. Savvy travelers can still spot those barns with certain English, German, French, or Spanish ancestry as they move across the countryside, particularly while following smaller dirt and gravel roads. But even as the old structures reveal their migration stories, they also entail in varying degrees narratives of an Americanizing process. In many of these buildings one can discover evidence of adjustment, improvement, and invention, changes enacted in order to help a barn better serve the aims of its owner.

The English barn provides a clear example of an instance of modernizing, of an updating of customary practices. In England a barn was used solely for storing threshed grain. The linguistic origins of the very word "barn"—a combination of two old Saxon words, "bere" (barley) and "aern" (place)—indicate that such a building was meant to serve only as a warehouse. The English farm featured an ensemble of many small and modest-sized buildings that might include a stable, cow house, sheep pen, cart shed, and hay barn as well as various sheds.[12] British settlers to New England, sensing a pressing need both for a more efficient arrangement and greater economy in the use of resources and labor, hit on the idea of consolidating the traditional set of farm buildings into one large structure.[13] They transformed their old grain warehouse into a multifunctional barn that contained spaces for stabling cows and horses, storing hay, threshing and storing grain, as well as places for keeping tools and other necessary equipment. Their new barns still looked old-fashioned when viewed from the outside because they retained the balanced symmetry of a central door flanked by storage areas of more or less equal size. Their innovations were confined chiefly to the interior with livestock penned on one side, their feed across the runway, and modest supplies of threshed grain kept overhead in the loft. The new English barn, old in appearance but new in its manner of operation, was simultaneously traditional and innovative, conservative and progressive. It offers a model of how many groups of settlers became Americans. They used their inherited pasts as a necessary resource but gradually modified what they remembered when faced with new demands and circumstances. Gradual pragmatic changes led not only to the emergence of new barns but to new identities.

Interactions between communities of German and English farmers in southeastern Pennsylvania offer an example of another mode of agricultural adaptation in the United States. Here the English borrowed elements of barn design from their German neighbors. Both groups came to America with plans for two-level bank barns in which a large grain store and hay barn stood above a stable for animals (compare 3-059 with 3-086). The key difference was that in the German barns extra storage space was gained by extending the front wall of the upper level 4 to 8 feet beyond the stable on the ground level. The resulting overhang, or forebay, gave these barns a very distinctive appearance. Some time around 1790 English farmers in and around Chester County began to modify their barns by adding a storage room to the front of the building.[14] While they replicated the German forebay in placement and function, these additions (called straw rooms) were so wide that they had to be supported by a set of substantial posts or masonry pillars (see 3-067–3-074). As with most cases of cultural borrowing, the process was not merely an act of copying. Rather, the English farmers observed and studied the advantages of German barns and then modified their own barns by adding a new feature that the Germans may have seen as awkward and ungainly. But the new barn type became popular and barns with posted forebays have been observed as far west as Illinois.[15]

In the Dutch-settled regions of New York and New Jersey the older barns were roughly square in plan with steeply pitched roofs and gable entrances that opened on to wide central threshing floors (see 3-008–3-018 for examples). In many respects these buildings resembled an ancient barn type from the Netherlands known as *Los Hoes* or *Einhaus*, which sheltered a farmer's family and his animals.[16] But in America animals and people were housed in different structures, a clear indication that a new cultural order focused on greater economic specialization was on the rise. While the abandonment of the old house-barn was an important change, during the 1830s many Dutch barns underwent an even more radical transformation when their roofs were rotated 90 degrees. Barns modified in this way had their entrances along their sides rather than at their gable ends (3-019).[17] Because the new barns also had narrower passageways, there was more space for stables that were needed to accommodate larger dairy herds. Moreover, since the new roof was raised several feet, there was also increased storage capacity in the loft. These renovations allowed a new generation of Dutch farmers to participate more aggressively in the expanding market for meat and dairy products required to feed the cities of the northeast. While they did not completely abandon their traditional barn structure, their extensive alterations to its roof and adjustments to its frame certainly changed the barn's visual form as well as the way that it was used.

Sometime between 1790 and 1810 cattle farmers living near the headwaters of the Holston River in eastern Tennessee found that they needed a larger barn that could both shelter their sizable herds and hold enough hay to get them through the winter.

Ancestral traditions offered only a set of small barns composed of log cribs.[18] The single-crib barn had been adequate at first; when a larger structure was needed either sheds were added to the crib or a second crib was added to the first. The double-crib barn, with its two storage areas arranged on either side of a central passage, was essentially a mountain version of the English three-bay barn (compare 5-025 with 4-018a). A four-crib was eventually developed by placing one double-crib barn behind another. While these barns provided more storage capacity, they also had two passageways—one running front to back and the other from side to side—and thus the design was flawed because valuable space was wasted (see 5-033).

After experimenting with this set of inadequate buildings, the farmers of far-eastern Tennessee developed a new barn type. Now called by scholars a transverse-crib barn, this structure contains at least six cribs arranged symmetrically on either side of a central passage running from one gable end to the other (see 5-046 and 5-047). In plan and dimensions, we could say that it was a four-crib barn with its eaves-side passageways closed off. However, this change resulted in a thorough transformation because a longitudinal plan was substituted for a lateral one.[19] The new barn offered farmers an efficient plan that also allowed easy expansion. With rows of stalls readily accessible to the central passage and supplies of feed located overhead in a vast hay mow or loft, the barn would become the most common type in Appalachia and eventually be accepted throughout the upland South. Because variants of this barn would eventually become a commonplace farming structure in the Midwest—the nation's most productive agricultural region—one can argue that it became the typical American barn, at least during the first half of the twentieth century (see 6-029–6-061).[20]

Inherited customs were the prime factor in the choice of barn design until the middle of the nineteenth century. But the invention of labor-saving tools and devices encouraged a reevaluation of traditional barn designs. A spirit of modern reform was also promoted by the writings of various building designers who advocated new farm plans based on the emerging field of agricultural science. In 1852 Lewis Allen, a cattle breed-

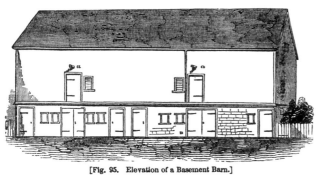

[Fig. 95. Elevation of a Basement Barn.]

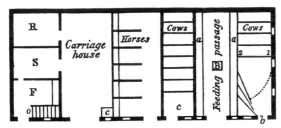

[Fig. 96. Plan of the Main Floor.]

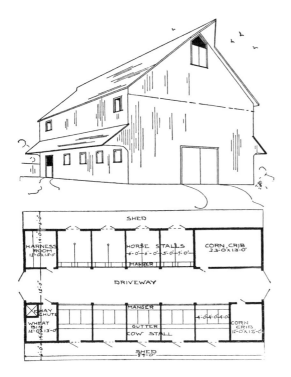

[Fig. 97. Plan of the Basement Floor.]

IN-016

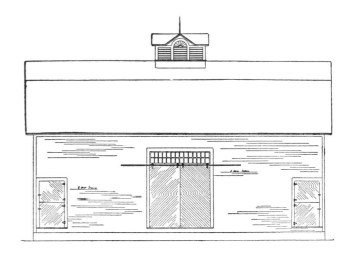

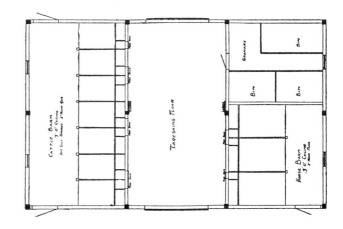

IN-017

IN-018

IN-019

IN-016. Figs. 95–97, from Andrew Jackson Downing, *The Architecture of Country Houses* (1850). Gen. Coll.

IN-017. Small farm barn, elevation, and floor plan, from William A. Radford, *Radford's Practical Barn Plans* (Chicago: Radford Architectual Company, 1909). Gen. Coll. This barn is a version of the standard English three-bay barn (see also 1-018–1-024; 4-018–4-021; 4-053–4-060; 5-033–5-036; 6-014; 8-020–8-024; 9-024 and 9-025).

IN-018. Barn from Mt. Carmel, Illinois, perspectival sketch and floor plan, from William A. Radford, *Radford's Practical Barn Plans*. This very typical transverse-crib barn was the dominant farming structure in the Midwest (see 6-031–6-061).

IN-019. Pole barn from Coshhocton County, Ohio. Allen G. Noble, photographer.

er from western New York, published a popular guide entitled *Rural Architecture, Being a Complete Description of Farm Houses, Cottages, and Outbuildings*, which included ideal plans for entire farms.[21] But the most popular architectural advisor was Andrew Jackson Downing, one of the nation's first landscape architects. In his book *The Architecture of Country Houses* (1850) he included a chapter, "Hints for Cottage and Farm Stables," in which he suggested how farms might be organized in a more efficient manner. One option was an array of different structures that he called a "Farmery," which consisted of eight different sheds and barns reserved for cattle, sheep, hogs, and grain, all tightly arranged around an interior courtyard. But the barn type that he admired most proved to be a traditional bank barn (IN-016). Of this building, which belonged to a farmer who lived just outside of Newburgh, New York, Downing wrote, "We have never seen, however, in any part of the country, a single farm building in which economy of space, excellence of arrangement, and nicety of construction were more completely combined than in this barn."[22] That old forms could contest with modern innovations indicates that older vernacular forms might be successfully adapted to serve farmers' needs even in an era of marked change. Between 1907 and 1917 editions of William A. Radford's *Practical Barn Plans* repeatedly advocated the construction of traditional three-bay, bank, and transverse-crib barns (IN-017 and IN-018).[23]

In the 1930s a corporate strategy for farming was developing out in southern California—the first portent of the system we now know as agribusiness. Under the new California scheme thousands acres of land were assembled by purchase or lease. With the operation headquartered in some distant city, these large farms were run by teams of management experts who directed gangs of nonresident workers hired on short seasonal contracts. Because the goal of the corporations was the extraction of as much productivity from the land as possible, concerns for family pride, community identity, or local history were supplanted by the profit motive.[24] These corporate estates, now operating throughout the country—and especially dominant across the South—are essentially outdoor factories. That the barns on these properties resemble the sorts of storage sheds and warehouses seen at textile and steel mills (9-045) is not too surprising. Called "pole barns," these standardized buildings are raised on grids of thin wooden poles that support prefabricated steel trusses. Covered with a skin of corrugated metal sheets, the barns are low and wide and topped by a roof with a very shallow pitch. Compared to other barns, these structures seem cold, mechanical, and faceless, like the corporations that spawned them. Of the pole barn geographer Alvar W. Carlson has noted: "Rarely are the whims of an individual builder or the ethnic background of a resident discernable."[25] That the pole barn is now becoming the structure of choice on the remaining family farms suggests the end of traditional barn designs in America.

BARNS ON THE LAND

Observing the path of the barn builder offers a precise way to outline the formation of succinct regional identities across the entire United States. Among the most durable elements of everyday life, barns reveal ethnic origins, mark the rise of new designs and construction techniques, and signal important shifts in their users' daily routines. If we may assume that old artifacts, like documents from earlier times, offer us messages about the past, then barns may "speak" as forcefully as the other forms of evidence on which we usually depend.[26] Anchored to the ground and often changed only slightly since the time of their construction, barns offer some assurance about what happened on a particular plot of ground. Surveying barns thus constitutes what might be called "above-ground archaeology."[27]

American barn types reveal the location of different thrusts of European settlement in the seventeenth and eighteenth centuries. All around the edges of the United States farm buildings mark the outlines of early settlement zones, places that geographers denote as "cultural hearths." It is in these various footholds that colonizing schemes took shape. Surviving barns in Massachusetts and Virginia reveal attempts to carry English ways to America (IN-016–IN-018; 4-005, 4-018a). Similarly, bank barns in southeastern

Pennsylvania show the influence of the German-speaking peoples who were invited to settle there by William Penn in order to provide other colonists with the positive example of their agricultural diligence (3-059–3-062). The distinctive hipped roof barns and other outbuildings of Louisiana speak to both the long reach of designs from Normandy and the adjustment to a tropical environment that the French had experienced first in the Caribbean before they reached the shores of the Gulf Coast (4-010, 4-042, 4-067a–4-067c). Beginning in the sixteenth century the long southwestern border, from Texas to California, was marked by four northward thrusts into what is today the United States. Some of the most visible results of these settlement efforts can be seen today in the farmsteads of northern New Mexico (7-015–7-025, 7-029–7-036) and southern California (9-007–9-016).

After the American war of revolution, there were important changes in agricultural practice. Various adjustments to life in the new land resulted in the development of new barn designs. Interaction between German and English farmers in the hinterland of Philadelphia, for example, gave rise to barns with large elevated "straw rooms" attached to one or more sides (3-067–3-074). In New England the old custom of scattering buildings about one's farm was, in the name of efficiency, gradually replaced with a layout that connected all the buildings into a tight cluster (IN-005–IN-013). The new farm plan was accompanied by the invention of a new barn with a gable entry and more efficient plan that replaced the old English threshing barn (IN-028–IN-031). Similarly the Dutch settlers of New York modified their barns by replacing their gable-entry barns with buildings with eaves-side doors (3-019). While all these changes were justified by claims of greater efficiency, we might also argue that the attraction of increased wealth encouraged a greater degree of individual choice. The decline of Old World traditions marked the rise of an American national character.

The southern mountains were a meeting ground for settlers moving west from the coastal plain of Virginia and south from Pennsylvania. One sign of the cultural synthesis forged between these two groups is found in log barns designed with cribs tall enough to provide hay storage above a stable (5-022–5-025), a feature that was probably adopted from the bank barns that Pennsylvania settlers built throughout the backcountry of Virginia (5-009, 5-063–5-065).[28] But the most important farming development in the southern highlands was the invention of the transverse-crib barn (5-037). While there are various explanations of the evolution of this barn type, there is no doubt that it swiftly became the dominant barn throughout the upland South.[29] Carried first into the lower Midwest, the transverse-crib barn would be adopted repeatedly by farmers all across the West as well. Well suited to ranches and farms raising cattle, horses, hay, or grain, the proven adaptability of the building's flexible design allowed this barn to become *the* American barn (see 6-031–6-056, 8-033–8-065, 9-026–9-041). As a regular feature of the landscape, the transverse-crib barn ties together much of the nation. Its geographical distribution closely parallels other broadly unifying patterns noted for regional dialect and vernacular music.[30]

During the last quarter of the nineteenth century barns designed at agricultural colleges were touted in numerous newspapers and trade magazines directed specifically at farmers. Meant to enhance increased levels of production, these buildings featured numerous innovations such as plank roof trusses, mechanical hay tracks, and improved ventilation and drainage systems. The most innovative of all these structures was the round barn devised in 1889 by Franklin H. King, a physics professor working at the Agricultural Experiment Station at the University of Wisconsin.[31] Some 90 feet in diameter, the barn had two levels. The stalls for the dairy cows on the ground floor were arranged around the perimeter of the barn, facing a large silo at the center of the building; the upper level provided storage space for a large supply of hay and straw. While the popularity of the round barn spiked dramatically about 1910, it fell quickly into disfavor. Even though these experimental barns were as efficient as promised, one scholar has observed, "our rectangular society has no room for a round structure."[32] While examples of round barns can be found in almost all regions of the United States, they are, finally, deviant buildings representing a momentary break with traditional designs (IN-

042, 2-009, 3-088, 3-089, 5-076, 6-082, 6-083, 9-042, 9-043). The public response to another barn designed at the University of Wisconsin is instructive. The so-called Wisconsin dairy barn was long and narrow in plan, often not more than 32 feet wide but frequently more than 100 feet in length (6-057–6-061).[33] Outfitted with a spacious hayloft, the barn had a ground floor arranged with two rows of milking stanchions divided by a narrow aisle. The building's longitudinal plan and gable entrance mimicked salient features of the older transverse-crib barn which had proved adequate during an era when the average dairy herd was considerably smaller (6-035). But increased demand for milk, cheese, and butter encouraged farmers to raise more cows and thus gave rise to a need for a larger barn. The Wisconsin dairy barn, even though it was a thoroughly modern building, gained widespread acceptance because it did not threaten or disrupt links to revered ancestral designs. Unlike the round barn, it did not break abruptly away from the past and thus it seemed a much safer choice. Traditions for barn design that had endured for centuries and over long distances proved too important to be simply discarded.

Only with the rise of an industrial mode of farming dependent on machinery, fertilizer, and insecticides to urge a crop from the soil were the links to traditional farming practices shattered. The scientific approach moved radically away from the ancient ideal of husbandry and its moral obligation to care for the land, to nurture and replenish it even as its bounty is taken. As the farmer became more and more of an engineer who forced nature to conform to his needs and his schedule, a new agenda was set for fields and pastures.[34] Instead of reading the signs of nature to gauge a farm's potential yield, the farmer read market reports and armed himself with the requisite tools and materiel needed to win from the land whatever he needed in order to turn a hefty profit. During the second half of the nineteenth century agricultural manuals referred to farms as businesses and workshops, a signal that bottom lines were becoming more important than bottom land. With this mode of thinking in place, it proved but a short step to the "farmerless farms" that would appear during the second quarter of the twentieth century.[35] Today, when the act of consumption is seen as more important than the work of production, it matters little what kinds of structures enable modern farmers to feed us. No longer can we expect to see the patient adjustments and experiments that once allowed older barns to serve new purposes. Now, when whatever works best at the least cost is good enough, a nondescript metal shed has become the barn of choice. Recently one historian has suggested that new farm machinery is the enemy not only of old barns, but of barns of any sort.[36] Indeed, all barns are out of place when fields are no longer seen as the source of our sustenance but as readily interchangeable agricultural units.

Now that we are well into the era of the computer chip we might think that concern for barns—things made of wood, brick, and stone—will soon fade to little more than dim nostalgic memories. Yet the responses to a traveling museum exhibition entitled "Barn Again!" reveals an enthusiasm for old farm buildings that is both deep and widespread. Launched in 1987, this exhibition moves back and forth across the country in an open-ended tour. In the process it is leaving in its wake a set of intriguing programs devoted to local barn research and rescue. The National Trust for Historic Preservation, in partnership with the magazine *Successful Farming*, annually offers a "Barn Again! Award" as a way of honoring the best efforts in preservation, restoration, or adaptive reuse. Ever mindful of their finances, the owners of these prizewinning old barns will quickly point out the economic argument for their actions: it costs much less to repair a broken barn than it does to build a new one. But they may also, on occasion, express deeper motives connected to personal identity and local history when they describe their barns as legacy buildings. Sensing in these structures a history of ancestral endurance and tenacity, they feel an obligation not to let these venerable buildings fall on their watch. While we cannot know how long the age of barns will last, now there are people enough who are willing to honor the past in a tangible way and thus ensure that some of the best barns will still be standing at the end of the twenty-first century.

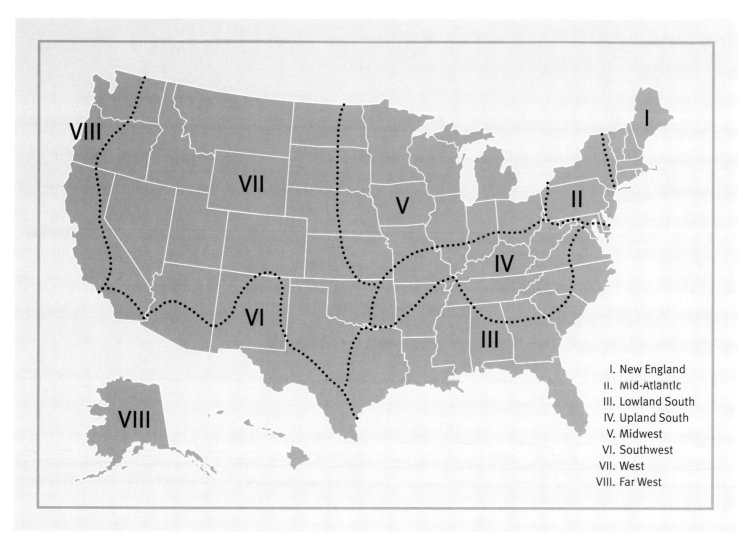

IN-020. Major cultural regions in the United States.

I. New England
II. Mid-Atlantic
III. Lowland South
IV. Upland South
V. Midwest
VI. Southwest
VII. West
VIII. Far West

WHILE THERE IS MUCH that can be learned by browsing through these assembled images, the photographs and drawings in *Barns* are arranged in order to convey a particular story of movement across time and space. Barns serve here as physical evidence of the key stages in American settlement history and as markers of specific pathways followed during the process of transcontinental migration. The flow of images runs from the eighteenth century to the twentieth and from the East to the West. Following the well-known settlement experience of Europeans in North America, we first observe various ethnic groups arriving at various places along the Atlantic shore and recreating, as best they can, farmsteads marked by the traditional buildings and agricultural practices of their original homelands. But when responding to challenging new circumstances, to matters both environmental and technological, a spirit of innovation develops that gives rise either to barns that are wholly new or to buildings that are significantly rearranged. Old barns that had once signaled an inherited ethnic identity are replaced by structures that mark the rise of new regional personalities. Dramatic changes occur as settlers move inland and different communities meet for the first time. In the upland South, for example, we witness the commingling of various regional barn designs and the rise of new, more useful models. The transverse-crib barn arises on this early western frontier from this sort of cultural encounter and eventually becomes the most common barn type all across the grain belt of the Midwest and the vast ranchlands of the western plains. While the Midwest also contained a number of ethnic "islands" marked by clusters of Germans, French, Scandinavians, and New Englanders, what emerges as dominant is a consensus regarding American agricultural practice. When we finally encounter the Far West, we recognize that the transverse-crib barn proves a highly adaptable building. While some new barn designs continue to appear—especially with the rise of agricultural science based at land grant colleges—it is clear that the transverse-crib became the dominant barn in the United States. It could be considered as the prime icon of the American farm.

Mixed in here with the numerous barns are examples of smaller agricultural structures such as stables, granaries, corncribs, and chicken houses. In some traditional schemes all of a farm's activities were gathered under the roof of a single large building. The bank barns of Pennsylvania, for example, provided space for crops, animals, workshops, and wagons and other equipment. But in the South each farming task was sheltered by its own structure so that a farm was effectively a village composed of little buildings. Given that a southern barn was often little more than a small pen of notched logs, we could accurately characterize a traditional southern farm as a collection of log barns (5-019). The samples of secondary farm structures included here help to present a full and accurate portrayal of the architecture of American agriculture. A barn strikes us as a dominant building in part because it is so often surrounded by a set of smaller structures. Collectively a barn and its associated outbuildings define the agricultural sector of the farm (see 5-004, 6-001). Standing somewhat aloof from the farm house, they suggest the truth of an old farmer's proverb: "A barn will build a house sooner than a house will build a barn."

NOTES

1. *Notes on the State of Virginia* (1787), ed. William Peden (Chapel Hill: University of North Carolina Press, 1955), 164.

2. John R. Stilgoe, *Common Landscape in America, 1580 to 1845* (New Haven: Yale University Press, 1982), 99–107.

3. John F. Kasson, *Civilizing the Machine: Technology and Republican Values in American, 1776–1900* (New York: Penguin Books, 1976), 6.

4. "Comfort for America, or remarks on her real situation, interests, and policy," *American Museum* I (1787): 6.

5. Stephen Daniels, *Fields of Vision, Landscape Imagery and National Identity in England and the United States* (Princeton: Princeton University Press, 1993), 177–78.

6. Cited in Irwin Unger, *These United States: The Questions of Our Past* (Englewood Cliffs, N.J.: Prentice Hall, 1989), 243.

7. Norman J. W. Thrower, "The County Atlas of the United States," *Surveying and Mapping* 21, no. 3 (1961): 365–73.

8. Henry Glassie, *The Spirit of Folk Art: The Girard Collection at the Museum of International Folk Art* (New York: Harry N. Abrams, 1989), 153.

9. David T. Stephens, "Midwest Barn Decor," in Allen G. Noble and Hubert G. H. Wilhelm, eds., *Barns of the Midwest* (Athens: Ohio University Press, 1995), 244.

10. "Bloch Brother's 75th Anniversary," *Building Blochs: Monthly Bulletin of the Bloch Brothers Tobacco Company* 3, no. 5 (1954): 1–2.

11. Brenda J. Boute, "Ads on Barns Still Crop Up," *Baltimore Sun*, April 13, 1999, 1-B.

12. R.W. Brunskill, *Illustrated Handbook of Vernacular Architecture* (London: Faber and Faber, 1971), 143–45; R.W. Brunskill, *Traditional Buildings of Britain: An Introduction to Vernacular Architecture* (London; Victor Gollancz, 1986), 58–59.

13. Henry Glassie, "Barns Across Southern England: A Note on Transatlantic Comparison and Architectural Meanings," *Pioneer America* 7, no. 1 (1975): 16–18; Robert Blair St. George, *Conversing by Signs: Poetic of Implication in Colonial New England Culture* (Chapel Hill: University of North Carolina Press, 1998), 108–10.

14. Robert F. Ensminger, *The Pennsylvania Barn: Its Origin, Evolution, and Distribution in North America* (Baltimore: The Johns Hopkins University Press, 1992), 87–93.

15. H. Wayne Price, "The Ground-Level, Posted-Forebay Barns of Brown County, Illinois," *Pioneer America Society Transactions*, 23 (2000): 1–14.

16. Theodore H. M. Prudon, "The Dutch Barn in America; Survival of a Medieval Structural Frame"

(1976), reprinted in Dell Upton and John Michael Vlach, *Common Places: Readings in American Vernacular Architecture* (Athens: University of Georgia Press, 1986), 209–11.

17. Greg Huber, "Ninety-Degree Roof Rotations in New Jersey Dutch Barns," *Material Culture* 31, no. 1 (1999): 1–21.

18. Henry Glassie, "The Old Barns of Appalachia," *Mountain Life and Work*, 40, no. 1 (1964): 21–25.

19. Terry G. Jordan-Bychkov, "Transverse-Crib Barns, the Upland South, and Pennsylvania Extended," *Material Culture*, 30, no. 2 (1998): 5–31. See also John Fraser Hart, *The Look of the Land* (Englewood Cliffs, N.J.: Prentice-Hall, 1975), 131–33, and Henry Glassie, *Pattern in the Material Folk Culture of the Eastern United States* (Philadelphia: University of Pennsylvania Press, 1968), 90–93.

20. Howard Wight Marshall, *Folk Architecture in Little Dixie: A Regional Culture in Missouri* (Columbia: University of Missouri Press, 1981), 72–77.

21. Mary M. Culver, "The Nineteenth Century Connected Farm: The Impact of Contemporary Printed Sources," *Pioneer America Society Transactions*, 18 (1995): 28.

22. Andrew Jackson Downing, *The Architecture of Country Houses*, 1850 (reprint, New York: Dover Publications, 1969), 218.

23. William A. Radford, *Radford's Practical Barn Plans, being a complete collection of practical, economical, and common-sense plans of barns, outbuildings and stock sheds*, 1908 (Chicago: Radford Architectural Company, 1908). This appeared in subsequent editions with slightly differing titles in 1909, 1911, 1914, 1915, and 1917. The numerous printings suggest both the enthusiasm for the book and the acceptance of the traditional plans that it contained.

24. Cary McWilliams, *Factories in the Field: The Story of Migratory Farm Labor in California* (Boston: Little, Brown, 1939), and Mark Kramer, *Three Farms: Making Milk, Meat, and Money from the American Soil* (New York: Bantam Books, 1977), 202–8. See also John B. Rehder, *Delta Sugar: Louisiana's Vanishing Plantation Landscape* (Baltimore: The Johns Hopkins University Press, 1999), 176–207, for an account of the spread of the California agribusiness model to Louisiana.

25. "Designating Historical Rural Areas: A Survey of Northwestern Ohio Barns," *Landscape* 22, no. 2 (1978): 32.

26. On the virtues of material culture as historical evidence see Henry Glassie, "Meaningful Things and Appropriate Myths: The Artifact's Place in American Studies," *Prospects* 3 (1977): 1–49; Ian M.G. Quimby, ed., *Material Culture and the Study of American Life* (New York: W. W. Norton, 1978); and Thomas Schlereth, ed., *Material Culture Studies in America* (Nashville: American Association for State and Local History, 1982).

27. The link between the practice of archaeology and the study of vernacular buildings was eloquently expressed by James Deetz in *Small Things Forgotten: The Archaeology of Early American Life* (Garden City, NY: Anchor Books, 1977), 92–117, 149–52.

28. Henry Glassie, "The Pennsylvania Barn in the South," *Pennsylvania Folklife* 15, nos. 2 & 4 (1965–66): 8–19; 12–25.

29. Terry G. Jordan-Bychkov, "Transverse-Crib Barns, the Upland South, and Pennsylvania Extended": 20–26; Henry Glassie, *Pattern in the Material Folk Culture of the Eastern United States*, 88–93.

30. The western distribution of the transverse-crib barn matches spatial patterns in language and folk song style. See John F. Rooney, Jr., Wilbur Zelinksy, and Dean R. Louder, eds., *This Remarkable Continent: An Atlas of United States and Canadian Society and Cultures* (College Station: Texas A&M University Press, 1982), 126, 238.

31. John T. Hanou, *A Round Indiana: Round Barns in the Hoosier State* (West Lafayette, Ind.: Purdue University Press, 1993), 13–14.

32. Hart, *The Look of the Land*, 136.

33. Allen G. Noble, *Wood, Brick, & Stone: The North American Settlement Landscape*, Vol. 2: *Barns and Farm Structures* (Amherst: University of Massachusetts Press, 1984), 45–46.

34. Stilgoe, *Common Landscape of America*, 164.

35. Kramer, *Three Farms*, 197–278.

36. Hanou, *A Round Indiana*, 32.

NEW ENGLAND

CONNECTICUT, MAINE, MASSACHUSETTS, NEW HAMPSHIRE, RHODE ISLAND, VERMONT

THE NEW ENGLAND REGION was not the most promising place to be a farmer. The soil was poor and the optimum growing season, the period between the last and first frosts, often amounted to less than fifteen weeks. New England farmers commonly joked that their fields pushed up more stones than plants. Yet, as these images suggest, bountiful farms appeared everywhere. Relatively small in size, to be sure, they manifest evident signs of success: cleared pastures, thriving herds, and substantial barns. These are the tangible proofs of a willingness to meet the challenges of a hard place with the requisite skills of husbandry and industry. New England farmers generally planted several types of grain to avoid the risks associated with raising only a single cash crop. Further, many households devoted a considerable portion of their day to home industries such as weaving, carpentry, metalwork, and the like. Sales of these crafted products combined with the produce of fields and herds allowed New England farmers to withstand the profound environmental challenges that they faced. A family's dwelling was then as much a sign of success as its barn.

1-001

1-001. Farm in Vermont. August, 1936. Carl Mydans, photographer. P & P, LC-USF 34-6909-D.

1-002. The Daigle farmstead near Fort Kent, Maine. August, 1942. John Collier, photographer. P & P, LC-USF 34-83721-C.

1-003. The Upway farm, Woodstock, Vermont. March, 1940. Marion Post Wolcott, photographer. P & P, LC-USZ61-2045.

1-002

1-003

NEW ENGLAND CONNECTED FARMS

Throughout the New England states occur clusters of farm buildings in which all the structures are connected to each other in either a straight row or a jagged line (compare 1-005 with 1-006). The sequence begins with the residence, leads progressively to a substantial kitchen wing through some kind of shed or shop, and ends with the barn. The general pattern is aptly captured by a nineteenth-century chant once sung as part of a children's counting out game: "Big House, little house, back house, barn."

Connecting all of a farm's buildings has often been explained as a clever local solution to the inconvenience of the region's high snow drifts that might block the farmer's path. It was alleged that if all the structures were attached, a farmer could move easily from house to barn without even going outside. However, careful research by architect Thomas C. Hubka reveals a more complex rationale. A host of reform movements—aesthetic, social, economic, architectural, religious—initiated in the region after 1850 culminated in a consolidated arrangement of the farm's buildings. Connection was seen by New England farmers as a sign of improvement that brought the domestic and the economic activities into a close and undeniable union.

1-004

1-004. Old red barn and farmhouse near Lowell, Vermont. August, 1936. Carl Mydans, photographer. P & P, LC-USF 34-6912-D.

1-005

1-006

1-007

1-005. Farmhouse and connecting buildings on the road to Sebago Lake, Maine. March, 1936. Paul Carter, photographer. P & P, LC-USF 341-2624-B.

1-006. Farm, Knox County, Maine. September, 1937. Arthur Rothstein, photographer. P & P, LC-USZ62-122729.

1-007. Farm buildings near Putney, Vermont. March, 1940. Marion Post Wolcott, photographer. P & P, LC-USF 34-53047-D.

opposite

1-008. The R. W. Cassidy farm near Putney, Vermont. February, 1940. Marion Post Wolcott, photographer. P & P, LC-USF 34-53030-D.

1-009. South elevation, Miles Cobb Farm House, 1788. Warren, Knox County, Maine. R. V. Keune and R. H. Swilley, delineators, 1960. P & P, HABS ME-76; HABS, ME,7-WAR, 1-, sheet no. 2, detail.

1-010. Plan, Miles Cobb Farm House, Warren, Knox County, Maine, 1788. James R. Redlogle, delineator, 1960. P & P, HABS ME-76; HABS, ME, 7-WAR, 1-, sheet no. 1.

1-011. Plan, William A. Farnsworth homestead, Rockland, Knox County, Maine. R. U. Keune and R. H. Swilley, delineators, 1960. P & P, HABS ME-77; HABS, ME, 7-ROCLA, 1-, sheet no. 1.

1-012. Benjamin Abbot farmhouse, Andover, Essex County, Massachusetts, 1685. Arthur C. Haskell, photographer, 1934. P & P, HABS MA-2-9; HABS, MASS, 5-ANDO, 1-3.

1-013. Site plan, Benjamin Abbot farmhouse, Andover, Essex County, Massachusetts. John R. Abbot, delineator, 1934. P & P, HABS MA-2-9; HABS, MASS, 5-ANDO, 1-, sheet 2.

Figure 1-013 and the two plans that precede it (1-010 and 1-011) reveal that layout of connected farm buildings could sometimes outline a discrete work space that was called a dooryard. Given the southern orientation of these farms, the collective mass of the adjoining buildings protected this area from the icy blasts of northern winds.

1-008

1-009

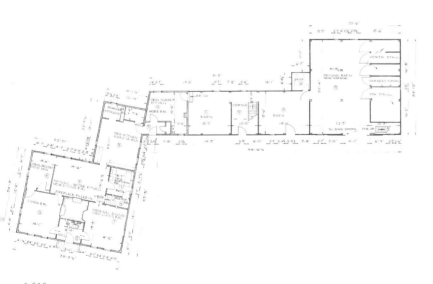

1-010

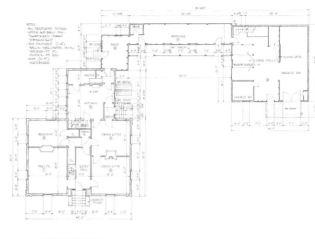

FIRST FLOOR PLAN
SCALE: 1/8" = 1'-0"

1-011

1-012

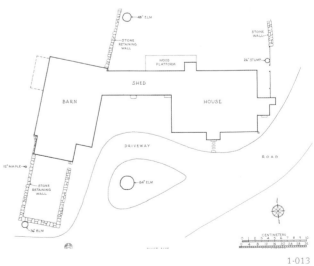

1-013

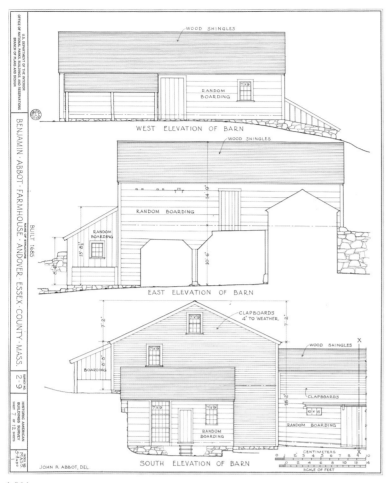

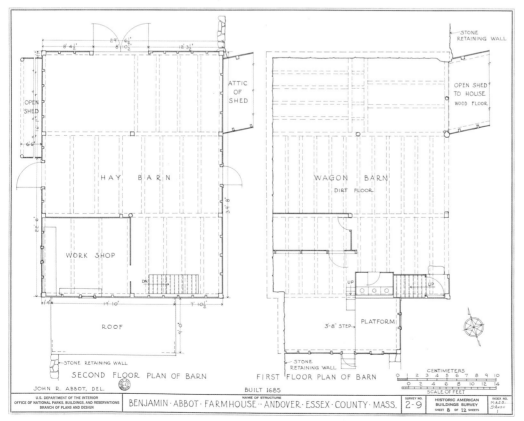

1-014. West, east, and south elevations, barn connected to the Benjamin Abbot farmhouse, Andover, Essex County, Massachusetts. John R. Abbot, delineator, 1934. P & P, HABS MA-2-9; HABS, MASS, 5-ANDO, 1-, sheet no. 8.

1-015. First and second floor plan for the barn connected to the Benjamin Abbot farmhouse, Andover, Essex County, Massachusetts. John R. Abbot, delineator, 1934. P & P, HABS MA-2-9; HABS MASS, 5-ANDO, 1-, sheet no. 9.

Taking advantage of the sloping site, Benjamin Abbot combined both a wagon barn and a hay barn in one structure by cleverly stacking one above the other. An interesting innovation, both are, in plan, good examples of the traditional three-bay English barn.

The three-bay barn is composed of three primary sections: a central wagon passageway flanked by two storage areas. Usually symmetrical in form (1-016, 1-017, 1-021), one side was sometimes built larger than the other in order to better serve a more specialized function. The hay storage bay, for example, might be larger than the section outfitted with cattle or horse stalls (1-016). The cultural source for New England's three-bay barns is easily traced to the British Isles, where the form has been in continuous use since the Middle Ages. Because the form is equally well known on the continent, the three-bay barns or granges encountered in the French-speaking areas of the St. John River valley of northern Maine should be credited to the influence of French agricultural traditions (1-019 and 1-020).

The three-bay barn remained a standard feature of New England farming. Its design was adequate for a small-scale multipurpose barn. When a larger barn was needed, carpenters might extend one end of the building with an additional bay or fashion a larger barn that was conceptually two three-bay barns side by side (1-023 and 1-024). Either strategy conservatively reinforced the utility of the old tradition.

1-016

1-017

1-016. John Nelson barn, Lincoln, Middlesex County, Massachusetts, ca. 1760. Jet Lowe, photographer, 1984. P & P, HABS MA-831-5; HABS, MASS, 9-LIN, 12-5.

1-017. Hargrove barn, Lexington, Middlesex County, Massachusetts, eighteenth century. Jet Lowe, photographer, 1984. P & P, HABS MA-1150; HABS, MASS, 9-LEX, 19-1.

1-018

1-018. Loading hay in a barn near Townsend, Vermont. 1941. Jack Delano, photographer. P & P, LC-USF 34-045229-D.

1-019. Hay barn on Leonard Gagnon's farm near Fort Kent, Maine. August, 1942. John Collier, photographer. P & P, LC-USF 34-083555-C.

1-020. Acadian barn near Madawaska, Maine. David A. Whitman, photographer, 1991. Maine Acadian Cultural Survey, AFC, LC, ME-DW-B019, no. 32.

1-021. South elevation and floor plan, Sylvanus Martin barn, Seekonk, Bristol County, Massachusetts. Philip A. Martineau, delineator, 1938. P & P, HABS MA-234; HABS, MASS, 3-SEKO, 2-, sheet no. 1.

1-019

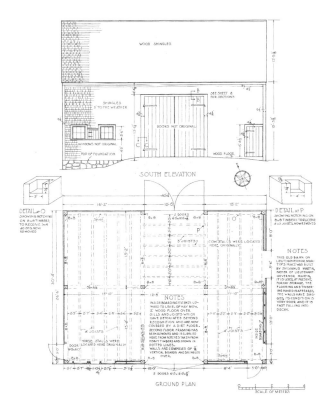

1-021

1-020

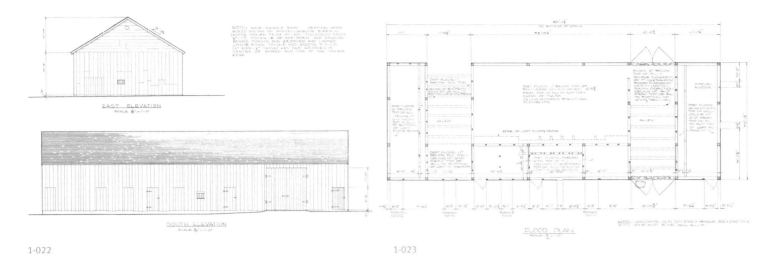

1-022

1-023

1-022. East and south elevations of the Hunt-Hosmer barn, Concord, Middlesex County, Massachusetts. Edward Bing, delineator, 1961. P & P, HABS MA-821, HABS, MASS, 9-CON, 16-, sheet no. 4.

1-023. Floor plan of the Hunt-Hosmer barn, Concord, Middlesex County, Massachusetts. Edward Bing, delineator, 1961. P & P, HABS MA-821; HABS, MASS, 9-CON, 16-, sheet no. 2.

1-024

1-024. Burbank-Hathaway barns and carriage house, Hartford County, Connecticut, nineteenth century. Robert J. Kelly, photographer, 1958. P & P, HABS CT-266; HABS, CONN, 2-SUFI, 7A-1.

BANK BARNS

While bank barns—two-level barns built into the slope of a hill—are most commonly linked to Germanic culture, an English tradition needs to be considered as well. In the so-called Lake Counties of northwestern England the bank barn is commonly encountered on farms devoted to raising cattle. It consists of a three-bay barn set atop a raised foundation; hay is stored in the upper section, above the animals. Unlike the German bank barn, in the English examples the upper portion does not overhang the lower stable area. Usually a long pent roof covers the entrances to the livestock stalls.

1-025

1-025. William Gaynor's dairy barn near Fairfield, Vermont. September, 1941. Jack Delano, photographer. P & P, LC-USF 34-45681-D.

1-026

1-026. Chase-Redfield barn, Randolph, Orange County, Vermont. Jack E. Boucher, photographer, 1960. P & P, HABS VT-54; HABS, VT, 9-RAND, 3A-1.

If a farm's topography was flat rather than hilly, as was the case with the Chase-Redfield farm, a ramp was built up to the second level.

1-027. Massachusetts barn. Carl Van Vechten, photographer, July, 1936. P & P, LOT 12736, no. 1338.

1-027

Gable-entrance barns made their appearance on the New England landscape around the middle of the nine-teenth century, replacing the venerable three-bay barn. The three-bay barn was an effective threshing "machine"; grain was beaten with flails in the barn's central passage. When the barn's front and rear doors were propped open, the central threshing floor was transformed into an efficient breezeway that effortlessly caused the useless chaff to be blown away. But with increased use of steam-powered threshing machines this activity was moved outside and the barn became a building reserved solely for storing hay. The long central floor of a gable-entrance barn allowed for easy loading and unloading, and this type of barn could readily be expanded without the need for an additional entry. The virtues of these efficiencies were not lost on canny New England farmers.

The new type was so widely and thoroughly accepted (no mean feat for a strongly traditional community) that it never acquired a name or label. Such structures are usually just referred to as "the barn." The rise in their popularity marks the shift from a dependence on ancestral patterns and wisdom to confidence in a new local invention.

1-028

1-028. Knowles barn, Lincoln, Middlesex County, Massachusetts. Cervin Robinson, photographer, 1963. P & P, HABS MA-793, HABS, MASS, 9-LIN, 10-1.

1-029. Jarathmael Bowers barns, Lowell, Middlesex County, Massachusetts. Frank O. Brancetti, 1941. P & P, HABS MA-525, HABS, MASS, 9-LOW, 4-2.

1-030. Dairy barn near Bristol, Rhode Island. August, 1936. Carl Van Vechten, photographer. Carl Van Vechten Collection, P & P, LOT 12736, no. 1387.

1-031. Barn at Maplewood Farm, New Hampshire. Detroit Publishing Company, 1900–1910. DPCC, P & P, LC-D4-15645 L.

1-029

1-030

1-031

NEW ENGLAND TOBACCO BARNS

Even though tobacco is usually considered a southern crop, the central Connecticut River valley has been a strong tobacco producing area as well. New England tobacco barns are distinctive mainly because of their narrow form, often extending as much as 100 feet in length. The harvested leaves are dried by the air flow that is directed throughout the building through numerous shutters. Given a short growing season and the early arrival of subfreezing temperatures, it is imperative that the tobacco cure quickly. The relatively thin profile of the New England tobacco barn ensures that the crop will be given maximum exposure to circulating air currents.

1-032

1-032. Tobacco barn, Agawam, Hampden County, Massachusetts, 1885. Arthur C. Haskell, photographer, 1937. P & P, HABS MA-151; HABS, MASS,7-AGAM, 3-1.

1-033. Floor plan, tobacco barn, Agawam, Hampden County, Massachusetts, 1885. Jacob B. Crytzer, delineator, 1935. P & P, HABS MA-151; HABS, MASS,7-AGAM, 3-, sheet no. 1, detail.

1-033

1-034a. South elevation, tobacco barn, Westfield, Hampden County, Massachusetts, 1855. Jacob B. Crytzer, delineator, 1935. P & P, HABS MA-103; HABS, MASS,7-WESFI,2-, sheet no. 1, detail.

This nineteenth-century barn was ventilated by hinging every other piece of vertical siding at the top and propping it open with a stick at the bottom.

1-034b. Floor plan, tobacco barn, Westfield, Hampden County, Massachusetts, 1855. Jacob B. Crytzer, delineator, 1935. P & P, HABS MA-103; HABS, MASS,7-WESFI,2-, sheet no. 1, detail

This barn is very similar to the example from Agawam, Massachusetts (1-033) but here the doors are located in the gable ends. The gable to gable alignment allowed the tobacco to be loaded or unloaded from the back of a wagon in one continuous process. The Agawam barn, divided into six equal units, each with its own entrance, was functionally six barns under one roof. Since each section had to be tended separately, the work proceeded at a considerably slower pace.

1-035. Tobacco barn near Greenfield, Connecticut. October, 1941. John Collier, photographer. P & P, LC-USF 34-80868-D.

Here the boards covering the barn were hinged along the sides and swung horizontally to open like conventional window shutters. The contrast with shutters that swing out from the top (1-036) is marked.

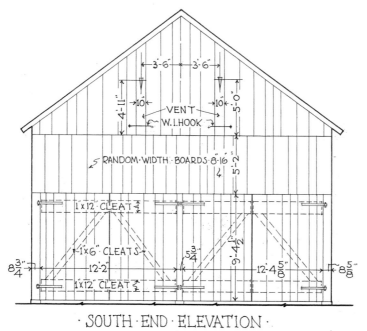

· SOUTH · END · ELEVATION ·

1-034a

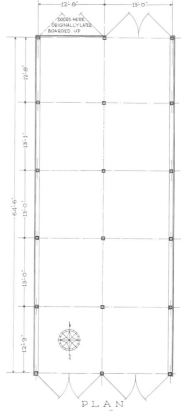

PLAN

1-034b

1-035

1-036

1-037

1-036. Tobacco barn near Thompsonville, Connecticut. September, 1941. Jack Delano, photographer. P & P, LC-USF 34-41554-D.

1-037. Tobacco field covered with cheese-cloth near Suffield, Connecticut. September, 1940. Jack Delano, photographer. P & P, LC-USF 34-041565-D.

Acres of cloth supported on long wires held up by many poles were a distinctive feature of Connecticut River valley tobacco landscape. The cloth shaded the leaves and kept them from turning brown before they were placed in the barn; it also suppressed attacks by certain varieties of insects.

OTHER NEW ENGLAND BARNS

1-038. Section and floor plan, Benjamin Dyer barn, Truro, Barnstable County, Massachusetts, mid-nineteenth century. Ralph H. Fertig, delineator, 1962. P & P, HABS MA-698; HABS, MASS, 1-TRU, 10- , sheet no. 2.

This small barn from circa 1850 was framed in the manner of a cottage with a low loft. Square in plan, the barn sheltered various agricultural routines with spaces allotted for a horse, two cows, coal and grain storage, and work space.

1-039. Potato barn near Caribou, Maine. 1940. Jack Delano, photographer. P & P, LC-USF 34-041825-D.

Potato barns were semi-subterranean structures built into the ground to ensure that potatoes would stay cool and not rot before they were shipped to market. More recent examples made with thick concrete walls work just as well and can stand fully above ground (see 1-041).

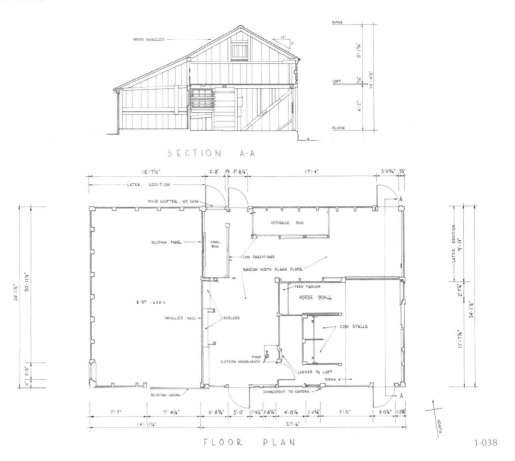

1-038

1-039

1-040

1-040. Potato barn near Wallagrass, Maine. Howard Wight Marshall, photographer, 1991. Maine Acadian Cultural Survey, AFC, LC, HM-B008, no. 11.

1-041. Herman Deprey's potato barn near St. Agatha, Maine. Howard Wight Marshall, photographer, 1991. Maine Acadian Cultural Survey, AFC, LC, HM-B016, no. 8.

1-042. Round barn in Caledonia County, Vermont, 1937. Arthur Rothstein, photographer. P & P, LC-USF 34-25487-D.

Enthusiastically promoted by agricultural reformers during the late nineteenth century as a prudent building design for efficient farming, the round barn was built all over the United States but never in great numbers. Despite all the enthusiasm of its promoters, it remained an experimental form that could not displace forms rooted in ethnic and regional traditions. (See also 1-004, 2-009, 3-088 and 3-089, 5-076, 9-042 and 9-043.)

1-041

1-042

1-043. Twin barn near St. Agatha, Maine, 1991. Howard Wight Marshall, photographer. Maine Acadian Cultural Survey, AFC, LC, HM-B105, no. 21.

This Acadian twin barn suggests the way that traditional patterns provide the model as well as the material for cultural innovation. Farmers of the St. John River Valley, finding their standard grange (the French version of the three-bay barn) no longer large enough to serve their needs, hit upon the idea of building two three-bay barns back to back and linking them with a short "hyphen." The result was a commodious but compact building with a distinctive M-shaped roof line. When Americans of English descent faced this same problem, they opted to link two barns end to end.

1-044. Twin barn near Hamlin, Maine. 1991. David Whitman, photographer. Maine Acadian Cultural Survey, AFC, LC, DW-B009, no. 9.

1-045. House and barn combined in one building near Andover, Massachusetts. January, 1941. Jack Delano, photographer. P & P, LC-USF 33-020799-M4.

This unusual building appears to be a barn that has had one end (the section closest to the public street) modified into a residence. The resulting house-barn recreates a building type well known in ancient Europe and brought to the United States by various groups of German immigrants who settled in the Midwest (see also 6-079 and 6-080).

1-043

1-044

1-045

Farmers generally kept their horses in the barn along with their other livestock and crops. Those who owned enough to fill an entire barn might have called that structure a stable, but the building would have had few outward signs of its more specialized use. All of the images in this section are from cities and towns. While not part of the agricultural landscape, they indicate that during the horse-drawn age urbanites as well as farmers had to make a place for barns in their domestic routines.

1-046

1-046. Eli Whitney Armory barn, Hamden, New Haven County, Connecticut, 1816. July, 1974. David Sharpe, photographer. P & P, HAER CT-2A-1; HAER, CONN, 3-HAM, 2A-1.

1-047. East, west, and south elevations, John Robinson stable, Salem, Essex County, Massachusetts, 1825. W. J. Livesy, delineator, 1936. P & P, HABS MA-208; HABS, MASS, 5-SAL, 23D-, sheet no. 3.

EAST ELEVATION   WEST ELEVATION   SOUTH ELEVATION

1-047

1-048. North, south, east, and west elevations, Sachem Street barn, New Haven, New
Haven County, Connecticut. Delineator
unknown, 1956. P & P, HABS CT-229; HABS,
CONN, 5-NEWHA, 24-, sheet no. 2.

1-049. Plot plan for the Gaoler's Barn,
Newburyport, Essex County, Massachusetts,
1825. Bernard Boisclair, delineator, 1934.
P & P, HABS MA-121; HABS, MASS, 5-
NEWBP, 19-, sheet no. 1.

NORTH (STREET) ELEVATION

WEST ELEVATION

SOUTH ELEVATION

EAST ELEVATION

1-048

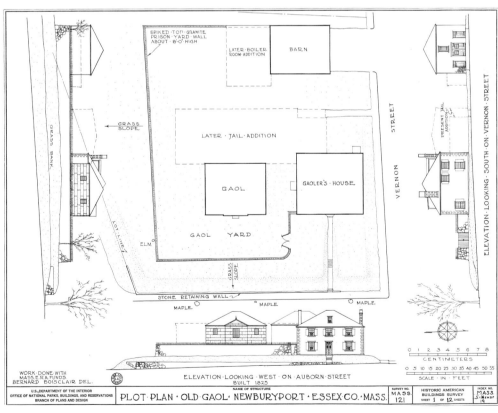

1-049

1-050

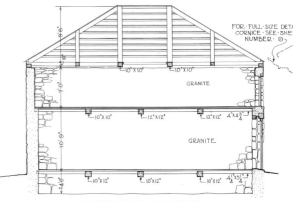

LONGITUDINAL · SECTION

1-053a

1-051

PLATE SECTION
AT · Y

G - G

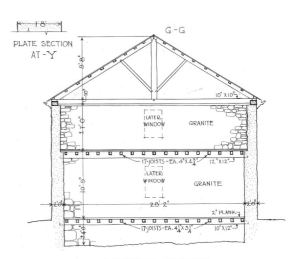

TRANSVERSE · SECTION

1-053b

1-052

1-050. Northeast view of the Gaoler's Barn, Newburyport, Essex County, Massachusetts. Arthur C. Haskell, photographer, 1934. HABS, MASS, 5-NEWBP, 19-6.

1-051. Stable, Guyot-Horsford House, Cambridge, Massachusetts, 1882. George M. Cushing, photographer, 1969. P & P, HABS MA-1021; HABS, MASS, 9-CAMB, 20-4.

1-052. First Parish Church stables, Lancaster, Worcester County, Massachusetts (view of the northern end). Jack E. Boucher, photographer, 1988. P & P, HABS MA-542-A ; HABS, MASS, 14-LANC, 1-A-3.

1-053a. Logitudinal section, Gaoler's Barn, Newburyport, Essex County, Massachusetts, 1825. Bernard Boisclair, delineator, 1934. P & P, HABS MA-121; HABS, MASS, 5-NEWBP, 19-, sheet no. 12, detail.

1-053b. Transverse section, Gaoler's Barn, Newburyport, Essex County, Massachusetts, 1825. Bernard Boisclair, delineator, 1934. P & P, HABS MA-121; HABS, MASS, 5-NEWBP, 19-, sheet no. 12, detail.

OUTBUILDINGS

No farm could operate effectively without a full com-
plement of outbuildings. Many of these structures,
such as the smokehouse, icehouse, woodshed,
and outdoor bake oven, were primarily associated
with the home but others, like the chicken coop,
hog sty, and granary, were devoted to agricultural
pursuits. Advocates for scientific agriculture like
William Radford might argue that all aspects of farm
work should for efficiency be gathered into a single,
centralized complex. But traditionalists countered
by holding on to their numerous and varied outbuildings that still seemed to work well enough.

1-054

1-055

1-054. Chicken house near Kirby, Vermont. September, 1937.
Arthur Rothstein, photographer. P & P, LC-USF 34-25785-D.

1-055. Chicken house near Jewett City, Connecticut. August, 1942.
John Collier, photographer. P & P, LC-USF 34-83844-C.

1-056. Woodshed in Lisbon, New Hampshire. March, 1940. Marion
Post Wolcott, photographer. P & P, LC-USF 34-53361-C.

This shed served several functions. It not only kept the firewood
dry and ready to use but also provided storage space for cattle
feed. The lean-to on the right served as a corncrib.

1-056

SHAKER

NORTHEAST AND BEYOND

COMMUNITIES

IN 1776 "Mother" Ann Lee and a small group of followers arrived in Niskayuna, New York, a small settlement near Albany. Lee was an early convert to a millennial sect known as the "Shaking Quakers" because of the frenzied movements observed in their religious services. While Lee's group called themselves the United Society of Believers in Christ's Second Appearing, they were known simply as the "Shakers." Proclaiming that Christ's second coming had already occurred, they set out to demonstrate how the promise of spiritual redemption could be lived in this world rather than in the next. Toward this end, the Shakers developed a series of what might be most accurately termed demonstration communities. Between 1780 and 1826 some twenty-five Shaker villages were established in New York, across New England, and as far west as Indiana and Kentucky. Numbering as many as 17,000 members, the Shakers made a notable and lasting imprint on the rural landscape of the northeastern United States. As such, they provide a tangible linkage between the New England and Mid-Atlantic regions.

While the number of practicing Shakers declined precipitously after 1860, a small community still survives at Sabbathday Lake, Maine.

Shaker architecture is noteworthy for its plain style and the evident efficiency of its design. Mother Ann was said to have counseled her followers to "Do your work as if you had a thousand years to live and as if you were to die tomorrow." This combination of urgency and diligence, bold action and careful planning, shows up clearly in the creation of Shaker barns. These buildings were the most exemplary farming structures of the nineteenth century. Impressive in their scale, construction, and mode of operation, they offered object lessons to all farmers interested in optimizing production.

COMMUNITY VIEWS

Views of Shaker villages produced by members of the sect offer intriguing insights about how the Shakers saw the world around them. These images are all the more interesting when we realize that the ascetic Shakers had no place for works of art in their lives. In 1845 they even declared a prohibition on "pictures or paintings set in frames within glass before them." Whatever urge to draw and paint Shaker men may have possessed had to be channeled into useful documents such as village maps. These documents were brilliantly colored, with red roofs, yellow walls, and green trees, but they were seen as serving mainly a useful function. Consequently, they were judged as acceptable even though they were, in fact, pictures. Present in all of them are a variety of barn types: three-bay barns, bank barns, and massive gable-entrance barns. As contemporary photographs show, many of these structures are still standing.

opposite
2-001. The Church Family at Harvard, Massachusetts. Charles Priest, 1833. G & M, Neg. #1670.

This village map, like most Shaker drawings, presents three-dimensional buildings as if they were lying flat on the ground. This blend of perspective sketching and cartography may have evolved as a technique for suppressing the pictorial or artistic character of an image.

2-002. Sketches of the Various Situations at Union Village (Ohio). George Kendall, 1835. G & M, Neg. #2297.

2-003. Diagram of the South Part of Shaker Village, Canterbury, N.H. Peter Foster, 1849. G & M, Neg. #1887.

Careful not to present himself as artist, Peter Foster added an apology in the corner of his "diagram" stating that he was "not . . . acquainted with any rules of drawing."

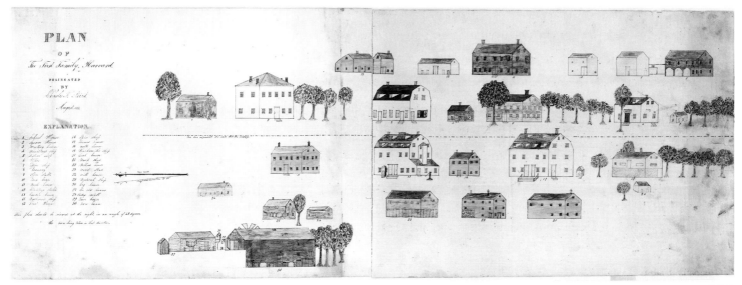

2-001

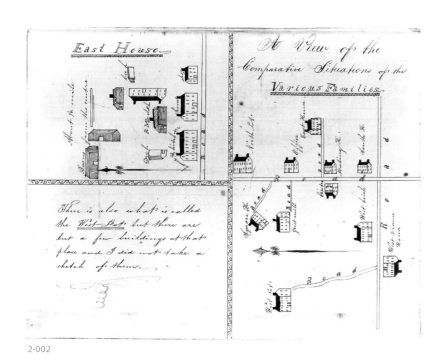

2-002

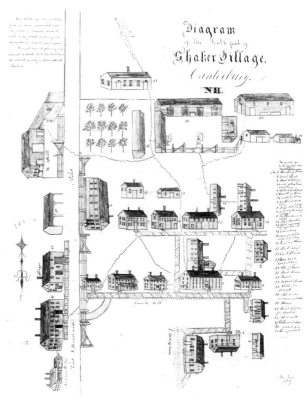

2-003

2-004

2-005

2-004. The Church Family at Alfred, Maine. Attributed to Joshua H. Bussell, ca. 1880. G & M, Neg. #1507.

Created when the Shaker membership was rapidly falling, this image reveals a definite weakening in the prohibition against works of art. Joshua Bussell produced several complex bird's-eye perspective views. He may have been guided by numerous printed views of towns that were in wide public circulation. Whether there is any special significance to the fact that three barns stand out prominently in the foreground may never be known. Yet it is interesting that he chose to emphasize the buildings for which the Shakers were most widely praised.

2-005. Shaker Church Family frame barn, Hancock, Berkshire County, Massachusetts. Elmer R. Pearson, photographer, 1971. P & P, HABS MA-1083; HABS, MASS, 2-HANC, 5-1.

In choosing a typical three-bay plan for this barn, the Shakers showed that they participated fully in the customary practices of local farming traditions even as they followed their own moral path.

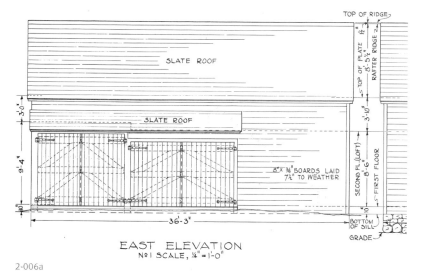

EAST ELEVATION
Nº1 SCALE, ¼" = 1'-0"

2-006a

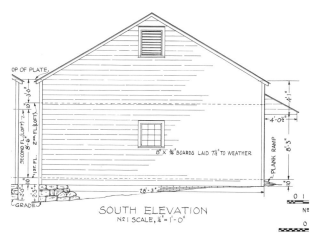

SOUTH ELEVATION
Nº1 SCALE, ¼" = 1'-0"

2-006b

2-006a. East elevation, Shaker South Family horse and wagon barn, Watervliet, Albany County, New York. L. G. Wands, delineator, 1941. P & P, HABS NY-3244; HABS, NY, 1-COL, 21-, sheet no. 2.

2-006b. South elevation, Shaker South Family horse and wagon barn, Watervliet, Albany County, New York. L. G. Wands, delineator, 1941. P & P, HABS NY-3244; HABS, NY, 1-COL, 21-, sheet no. 2.

2-007. Church Family barns, Sabbathday Lake, Cumberland County, Maine. Miller/Swift, photographers, 1970. P & P, HABS ME-167; HABS, ME, 3-SAB, 2-1.

These gable-entrance barns represent a shift in barn designs during the second half of the nineteenth century. Compare with examples seen in 1-003 and 1-028–1-031.

2-007

2-008

2-008. Tyringham Settlement, ox barn, Tyringham, Berkshire County, Massachusetts. Jack E. Boucher, photographer, 1988. P & P, HABS MA-1238A; HABS, MASS, 2-TYR, 2-1.

Bank barns were used across New England but this Shaker example is special in two respects. It not only has three levels but the bridge entrance to the top level is quite long. Because this barn sheltered teams of oxen, the designer of the long bridge developed a wide landing adjacent to the second level so that the livestock could be more easily moved in and out. Compare with 3-076 and 3-088.

2-009. Shaker Church Family round barn, Hancock, Berkshire County, Massachusetts, 1826, rebuilt 1865. Jack E. Boucher, photographer, 1962. P & P, HABS MA-674; HABS, MASS, 2-HANC, 9-1.

Based on what was believed to be a divinely inspired plan, this unique Shaker barn was built in a circular configuration. The barn nevertheless functioned like any two-level hay barn where the feed was stored above the stock. On the lower level cows were gathered around the perimeter and faced inward. Above them on the second level was a narrow floor that allowed hay wagons to enter and travel all the way around the building as their loads were deposited into the center of the barn. The clerestory on the third level allowed adequate light into this capacious barn, almost 90 feet in diameter.

2-010. Interior of Shaker Church Family round barn, Hancock, Berkshire County, Massachusetts. Jack E. Boucher, photographer, 1962. P & P, HABS MA-674; HABS, MASS, 2-HANC, 9-16.

2-009

2-010

2-011. West elevation of the Shaker Church Family cow barn, Enfield Vic., Grafton County, New Hampshire, 1854. Patrick M. Burkhart, delineator, 1978. P & P, HABS NH-192; HABS, NH, 5-ENFI.V, 1B-, drawing no. 3.

Because Shaker farms were corporate ventures, it proved most efficient to shelter all production tasks in one or two large barns. These were typically multilevel structures measuring as much as 200 feet long.

2-012. Floor plan and south elevation of the Shaker Church Family cow barn, Enfield Vic., Grafton County, New Hampshire. Patrick M. Burkhart, delineator, 1978. P & P, HABS NH-192; HABS, NH, 5-ENFI.V, 1B-, sheet no. 2.

2-013. Shaker South Family barn, Harvard, Worcester County, Massachusetts. Stanley P. Mixon, photographer, 1940. P & P, HABS MA-808; HABS, MASS, 14-HARV, 10-7.

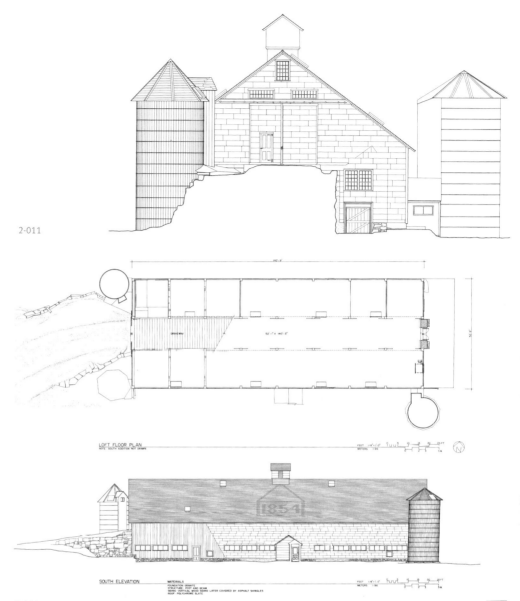

2-011

2-012

2-013

2-014

2-014. Shaker South Family cow and hay barn, Watervliet, Albany County, New York. Nelson E. Baldwin, photographer, 1939. P & P, HABS NY-3245; HABS, NY, 1-COL, 21-1.

2-015. Cross-section of the Shaker South Family cow and hay barn, Watervliet, Albany County, New York. G. Willoughby Allen, delineator, 1940. P & P, HABS NY- 3245; NY, 1-COL, 21-, sheet no. 6, detail.

2-016. North elevation of the Shaker North Family barn, Mount Lebanon, Columbia County, New York. A. K. Mosley, delineator, 1940. P & P, HABS NY-3215; HABS, NY, 11-NELEB.V, 30-, sheet no. 1, detail.

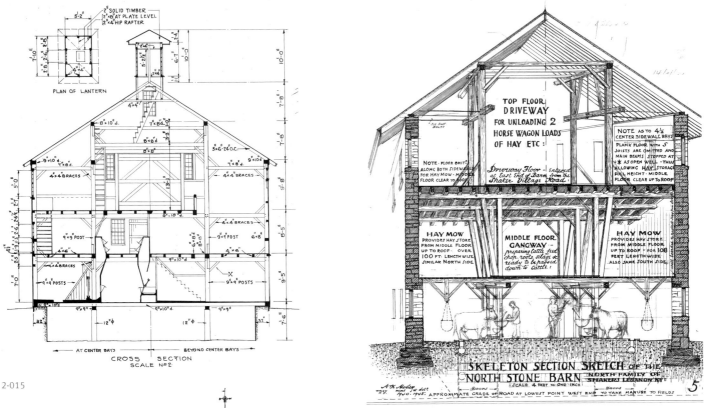

2-015

2-017

2-016

2-017. Skeleton sketch of the interior of Shaker North Family barn, New Lebanon, Columbia County, New York. A. K. Mosley, delineator, 1940. P & P, HABS NY-3215; HABS, NY, 11-NELEB.V, 30-, sheet no. 5.

2-018. Shaker Church Family concrete barn,
Hancock, Worcester County, Massachusetts.
Elmer R. Pearson, 1970. P & P, HABS MA-
1082; HABS, MASS, 2-HANC, 2-1.

That the large gable-entrance, multilevel
Shaker barn continued to be built into the
twentieth century is illustrated by this example, which is constructed in concrete.

2-019

2-019. Shaker Church Family barn and granary, Canterbury, Merrimack County, New Hampshire. Elmer R. Pearson, photographer, 1971. P & P, HABS NH-177; HABS, NH, 7-CANT, 1-1.

Shaker granaries, like barns, were large warehouses for field produce. Their immense size gave a Shaker village more of the appearance of a factory than a residential community. The long barn looms up in the background.

2-020. Shaker North Family granary, Mount Lebanon, Columbia County, New York. Nelson E. Baldwin, photographer, 1939. P & P, HABS NY-3320; HABS, NY, 11-NELEB.V, 34-1.

2-021. Shaker West Family barns, Pleasant Hill, Mercer County, Kentucky. Lester Jones, photographer, 1940. P & P, HABS KY-87; HABS, KY, 84-SHAKT, 13-1.

2-020

2-021

2-022. Shaker Centre barn, South Union,
Logan County, Kentucky. Elmer R. Pearson,
photographer, 1973. P & P, HABS, KY-104;
HABS, KY, 71-SOUN, 8-1.

The Shaker Centre barn takes the form of
a transverse-crib barn, a type dominant in
the upland South region. See section 5, fig-
ures 5-037–5-056, for a number of parallel
examples; especially 5-052 for its scale and
5-042 for its design. The Shaker community
in Kentucky seems to have followed the
local custom rather than initiating one of
their own. Yet this barn, like others constructed by the Shakers, is both large and
visually impressive.

THE MID-

DELAWARE, NEW JERSEY, NEW YORK, PENNSYLVANIA

ATLANTIC

MID-ATLANTIC FARMSCAPES

The Mid-Atlantic states, dominated by the rugged Appalachian mountain chain and its ridges, hills, and plateaus, contain some of the most productive farmland in the United States. Broad valleys cut by the Hudson, Mohawk, Susquehanna, and Delaware rivers are well known for their rich topsoil. Here a productive dairy industry thrived (3-001–3-003). In southeastern Pennsylvania success is readily indicated by the size of the capacious barns seen along nearly every country road (3-004 and 3-005). New Jersey (3-006 and 3-007) and Delaware stand for the most part atop the rolling coastal plain and, in addition to dairying, these states are known for fruit, vegetables, and poultry. Much of this production feeds the multitudes living in the adjacent metropolitan areas around Philadelphia and New York and continues to justify New Jersey's nickname, the "Garden State."

While the Mid-Atlantic developed under British control, the region was clearly marked by considerable ethnic diversity. During the eighteenth century counties in the hinterlands of Philadelphia were dominated by Germans and Ulster Scots. The Germanic presence continues to be indicated by distinctive two-level barns (3-005). Signs of the Dutch, the first Europeans to settle in the Hudson Valley, are also still visible on the land. The old Dutch farmsteads are marked by durable farmhouses, often built in stone or brick, and by distinctive wide, gable-entrance barns (3-007). Ensembles of Dutch houses and barns can be found across Long Island, through the northern counties of New Jersey, and as far north as the Mohawk Valley of New York.

3-001. Farm near Townsend, New York. September, 1940. Jack Delano, photographer. P & P, LC-USF 34-4147-D.

3-002. Farm in Otsego County, New York. September, 1937.
Arthur Rothstein, photographer. P & P, LC-USF 34-25892-D.

3-003. Dairy farm in Little Falls, New York. John Collier,
photographer, October, 1941. P & P, LC-USF34-81197-C.

3-004. Farm in Bucks County, Pennsylvania. June, 1939. Marion
Post Wolcott, photographer. P & P, LC-USF34-051994-D.

3-002

3-003

3-004

3-005

3-006

3-007

3-005. Farm in York County, Pennsylvania. June, 1939. Marion Post Wolcott, photographer. P & P, LC-USF 34-51965-D.

3-006. Farm near Lamington, New Jersey. 1945. Gottscho-Schleisner, Inc., photographer. P & P, LC-G612-T-48182.

3-007. De Clerque farm near Closter, Bergen County, New Jersey. R. Merrit Lacey, photographer, 1937. P & P, HABS NJ- ; HABS, NJ, 2-CLOST, 3-6.

For detailed drawings of the De Clerque barn see 3-016 and 3-017. The substantial corncrib, seen between the barn and the house, is illustrated in 3-105a–3-105c.

DUTCH BARNS

The Dutch barn stands apart from the English barn in several respects. It is nearly square in plan, rather than rectangular, with a wide central floor flanked by small stalls for animals. By contrast, the English barn features large stabling areas on either side of a smaller central passage. The high roof of the Dutch barn allows space for hay storage sufficient to last through a long winter. Also distinctive is its front-facing gable, an orientation that marks the building as belonging to a class of structures fully separate from the house that it accompanies.

3-008. Schermerhorn barn, Rotterdam, Schenectady County, New York. G. W. Allen and A. I. Delahanty, photographers, 1937. P & P, HABS NY-371; HABS, NY, 47-ROT, 2-4.

The steeply pitched roof and the low side walls seen in this building are representative of ancient barns in Holland. The angle of the rafters suggests either a barn of great antiquity or a carpenter guided by archaic ideals. The steep slope of the rafters is consistent with a roof that was intended to be covered with thatch. (Such roofs need to be very steep in order for them to shed water. A shallower pitch would cause the thatch to become waterlogged and the roof to collapse because of the extra weight.)

The Dutch living in New York and New Jersey universally covered their barn roofs with wooden shingles and thus found that the rafters could be set at a shallower pitch. This move allowed the side walls to be raised higher and the interior volume of the storage space in the loft to be increased considerably.

3-008

3-009

3-009. Johannes Decker barn, Shawangunk,
Ulster County, New York. D. M. C. Hopping,
photographer, 1970. P & P, HABS NY-6133;
HABS, NY, 56-SHWA, 3A-1.

3-010. Cross section of the Johannes Decker
barn, Shawangunk, Ulster County, New York.
D. M. C. Hopping, R. Fleury, delineators,
1970. P & P, HABS NY-6133; HABS, NY, 56-
SHWA, 3A-1.

This sectional diagram reveals the most distinctive structural trait of a Dutch barn. Its
central framing unit or *bent* is shaped like a
capital H. The middle bar of the H, called
the anchor beam, is very large so that it can
support the weight of a load of hay across
the span of the threshing floor. (See also
figs. 3-012a, 3-017, 3-025.)

CROSS SECTION
AT LINE "A-A"

SCALE 1/4" = 1'

3-010

3-011. Nicholas Haring barn, Rockleigh,
Bergen County, New Jersey. R. Merrit Lacey,
photographer, 1936. P & P, HABS NJ-169;
HABS, NJ, 2-NORVA, 1-12.

3-012a. Cross section, Nicholas Haring
barn, Rockleigh, Bergen County, New Jersey.
W. H. Stautmeister, delineator, 1935. P & P,
HABS NJ-169; HABS, NJ, 2-NORVA, 1-, drawing no. 11, detail.

3-012b. Floor plan, Nicholas Haring barn,
Rockleigh, Bergen County, New Jersey. W. H.
Stautmeister, delineator, 1935. P & P, HABS
NJ-169; HABS, NJ, 2-NORVA, 1-, drawing no.
11, detail.

3-011

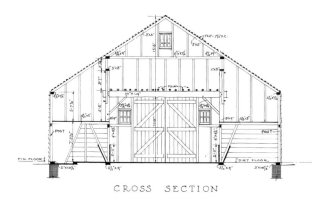

CROSS SECTION

3-012a

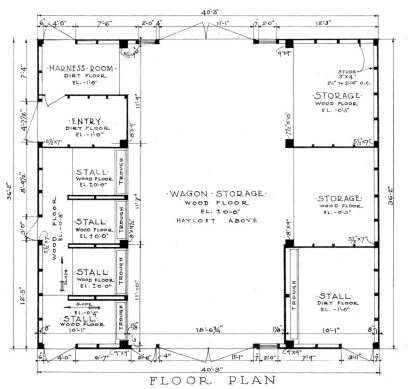

FLOOR PLAN

3-012b

NORTHEAST ELEVATION

3-013a

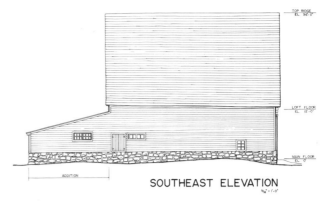

SOUTHEAST ELEVATION

3-013b

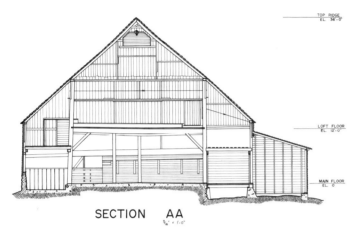

SECTION AA

3-014

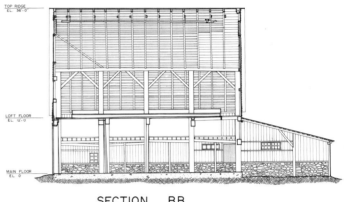

SECTION BB

ISOMETRIC OF STRUCTURAL FRAMING
SHOWING ORIGINAL HAND HEWN TIMBERS

VAN CAMPEN-DEWITT BARN
WALLPACK CENTER VICINITY   SUSSEX COUNTY   NEW JERSEY

3-015

3-013a. Northeast elevation, Van Campen-Dewitt barn, Wallpack Center Vic., Sussex County, New Jersey. Robert G. Giebener, delineator, 1967. P & P, HABS NJ-736; HABS, NJ, 19-WALPAC.V, 3-, drawing no. 3.

3-013b. Southeast elevation, Van-Campen-Dewitt barn, Wallpack Center Vic., Sussex County, New Jersey. Robert G. Giebener, delineator, 1967. P & P, HABS NJ-736; HABS, NJ, 19-WALPAC.V, 3-, sheet no. 3, detail.

3-014. Section, Van-Campen-Dewitt barn, Wallpack Center Vic., Sussex County, New Jersey. Dennis E. Walo, delineator, 1967. P & P, HABS NJ-736; HABS, NJ, 19-WALPAC.V, 3-, sheet no. 4, detail.

3-015. Isometric drawing of the structural framing of the Van-Campen-Dewitt barn, Wallpack Center Vic., Sussex County, New Jersey. David L. Bouse, delineator, 1967. P & P, HABS NJ-736; HABS, NJ, 19-WALPAC.V, 3-, sheet no. 5.

This drawing illustrates how the five central H-shaped bents of the Van Campen-Dewitt barn define the wide central threshing floor and support the rafters that in turn support the roof. The outer aisles, where the animal stalls are located, are basically appended to the outer edges of the central bents.

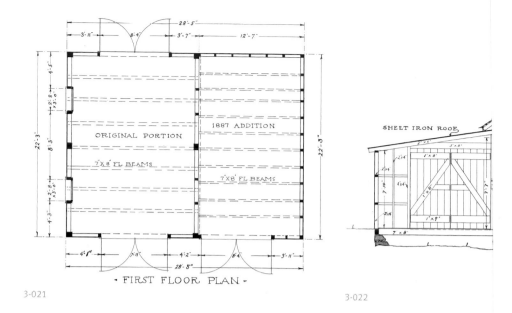

· FIRST FLOOR PLAN ·

3-021

SHEET IRON ROOF

3-022

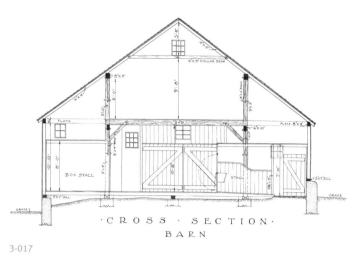

· NORTH · ELEVATION ·
BARN

3-016

· CROSS · SECTION ·
BARN

3-017

3-021. Plan, Banta barn, Paramus, Bergen County, New Jersey. Wallace Dunlop, J. D. Howard, delineators, 1935. P & P, HABS NJ-163; HABS, NJ, 2-PARA, 3- , sheet no. 7, detail.

3-022. Section, Banta barn, Paramus, Bergen County, New Jersey. Wallace Dunlop, J. D. Howard, delineators, 1935. P & P, HABS NJ-163; HABS, NJ, 2-PARA, 3- , sheet no. 8, detail.

3-023. Bird's-eye view of the Zabriskie farm, Paramus, Bergen County, New Jersey. Frederic Lansing, delineator, 1935. P & P, HABS NJ-157; HABS, NJ, 2-PARA, 2-, sheet no. 1.

Built in 1826, the Jacob Zabriskie farm was marvelously intact when documented more than century later. It provides a significant time capsule of the daily routine on a Dutch farm. In the agricultural section of the farmstead stood both a large and a small barn, grain and corncribs raised on stilts, plus a workshop and a number of miscellaneous sheds. All of these were captured in the following measured drawings (3-024– 3-027).

FREDERIC LANSING · DEL

· BIRD'S · EYE · VIEW · O

U.S. DEPARTMENT OF THE INTERIOR
OFFICE OF NATIONAL PARKS, BUILDINGS, AND RESERVATIONS
BRANCH OF PLANS AND DESIGN

NAME OF BUI
· THE · JACOB · ZABRISK
· SOUTH · PARAMUS · ROAD · BOROUG

3-016. North elevation, De Clerque barn, Closter, Bergen County, New Jersey. C. R. Johnson, delineator, 1937. P & P, HABS NJ-364; HABS, NJ, 2-CLOST, 3- , sheet no. 19.

3-017. Cross section, De Clerque barn, Closter, Bergen County, New Jersey. C. R. Johnson, delineator, 1937. P & P, HABS NJ-364; HABS, NJ, 2-CLOST, 3- , sheet no. 25.

3-018. Wemple barn, Dunsville, Albany County, New York. Nelson E. Baldwin, ca. 1936. P & P, HABS NY-3156; HABS, NY, 1-DUNV, 1A-1.

This conventional Dutch barn was modified with a ramp along one side providing direct access to the hayloft.

3-018

3-019

3-020

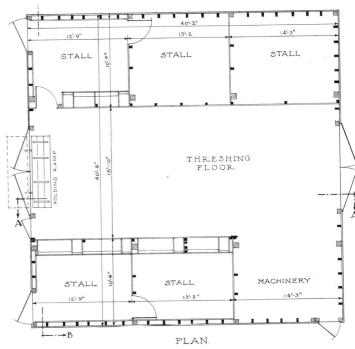

3-024

3-024. East, south, and north elevations and longitudinal section, Zabriskie barn, Paramus, Bergen County, New Jersey. Francis W. Schuman, Elizabeth Joan De Brezeni, delineators, 1935. P & P, HABS NJ-157; HABS, NJ, 2-PARA, 2-, sheet no. 8.

3-025a. Transverse section, Zabriskie barn, Paramus, Bergen County, New Jersey. F. W. Schuman, delineator, 1935. P & P, HABS NJ-157; HABS, NJ, 2-PARA, 2-, sheet no. 9, detail.

3-025b. Plan, Zabriskie barn, Paramus, Bergen County, New Jersey. F. W. Schuman, delineator, 1935. P & P, HABS NJ-157; HABS, NJ, 2-PARA, 2-, sheet no. 9, detail.

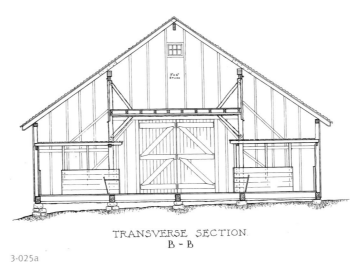

3-025a

3-025b

3-026a. North elevation of the workshop, sleigh house, and sheds at the Zabriskie farm, Paramus, Bergen County, New Jersey. G. E. Hazen, delineator, 1935. P & P, HABS NJ-157; HABS, NJ, 2-PARA, 2-, sheet no. 10, detail.

3-026b. Plan of the workshop, sleigh house, and sheds at the Zabriskie farm, Paramus, Bergen County, New Jersey. G. E. Hazen, delineator, 1935. P & P, HABS NJ-157; HABS, NJ, 2-PARA, 2-, sheet no. 10, detail.

3-026c. South elevation of the grain crib at the Zabriskie farm, Paramus, Bergen County, New Jersey. G. E. Hazen, delineator, 1935. P & P, HABS NJ-157; HABS, NJ, 2-PARA, 2-, drawing no. 10, detail.

3-026d. East elevation of the grain crib at the Zabriskie farm, Paramus, Bergen County, New Jersey. G. E. Hazen, delineator, 1935. P & P, HABS NJ-157; HABS, NJ, 2-PARA, 2-, sheet no. 10, detail.

3-026e. Plan of the grain crib at the Zabriskie farm, Paramus, Bergen County, New Jersey. G. E. Hazen, delineator, 1935. P & P, HABS NJ-157; HABS, NJ, 2-PARA, 2-, sheet no. 10, detail.

3-026a

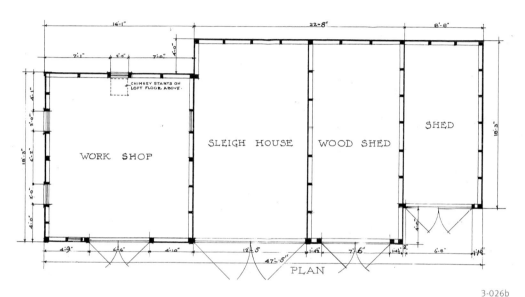

3-026b

3-026c

EAST ELEVATION

3-026d

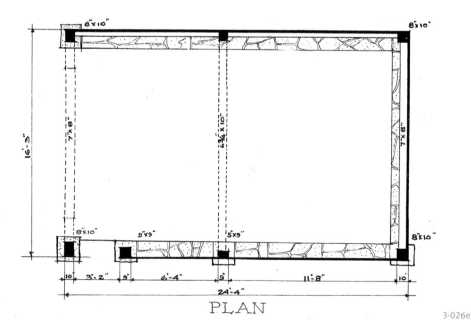

PLAN

3-026e

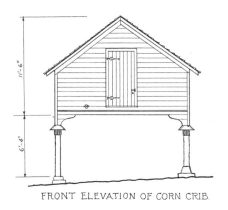

FRONT ELEVATION OF CORN CRIB.

3-027a

FRONT ELEVATION OF SMALL BARN

3-027d

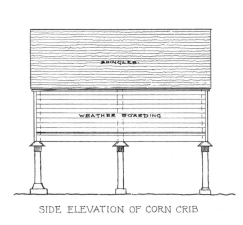

SIDE ELEVATION OF CORN CRIB

3-027b

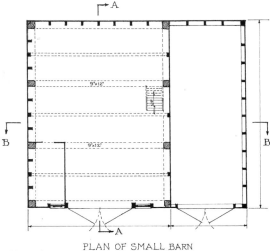

PLAN OF SMALL BARN

3-027e

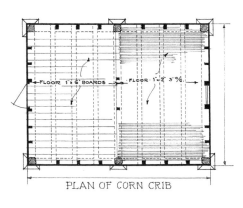

PLAN OF CORN CRIB

3-027c

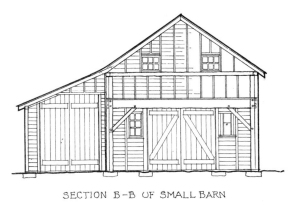

SECTION B-B OF SMALL BARN

3-027f

3-027a. Front elevation of the corncrib at the Zabriskie farm, Paramus, Bergen County, New Jersey. O. Brandenberger, delineator, 1935. P & P, HABS NJ-157; HABS, NJ, 2-PARA, 2-, sheet no. 11, detail.

3-027b. Side elevation of the corncrib at the Zabriskie farm, Paramus, Bergen County, New Jersey. O. Brandenberger, delineator, 1935. P & P, HABS NJ-157; HABS, NJ, 2-PARA, 2-, sheet no. 11, detail.

3-027c. Plan of the corncrib at the Zabriskie farm, Paramus, Bergen County, New Jersey. O. Brandenberger, delineator, 1935. P & P, HABS NJ-157; HABS, NJ, 2-PARA, 2-, sheet no. 11, detail.

3-027d. Front elevation of the small barn at the Zabriskie farm, Paramus, Bergen County, New Jersey. O. Brandenberger, delineator, 1935. P & P, HABS NJ-157; HABS, NJ, 2-PARA, 2-, sheet no. 11, detail.

3-027e. Plan of the small barn at the Zabriskie farm, Paramus, Bergen County, New Jersey. O. Brandenberger, delineator, 1935. P & P, HABS NJ-157; HABS, NJ, 2-PARA, 2-, sheet no. 11, detail.

3-027f. Section of the small barn at the Zabriskie farm, Paramus, Bergen County, New Jersey. O. Brandenberger, delineator, 1935. P & P, HABS NJ-157; HABS, NJ, 2-PARA, 2-, sheet no. 11, detail.

Note the exceptional width of the anchor beam for this small barn. Compared with the sectional drawing for the Banta barn (see 3-022), it suggests either the anticipation of heavy loads or the desire to construct a legacy building, one that would endure.

SINGLE-UNIT BARNS

The smallest barns consisted of no more than a small enclosure formed by four walls and a roof. Such buildings were usually erected in the first years of settlement and then either replaced as the farmstead grew or turned into secondary storage buildings.

3-028. Log barn at the Moore-Stiles farm, Lumberton Vic., Burlington County, New Jersey, ca. 1740. Nathaniel R. Ewan, 1937. P & P, HABS NJ-453; HABS, NJ, 3-LUMTO.V, 2A-4.

Both this log barn and the stone one (3-030a–3-030c) were outfitted as stables.

3-029. Log barn, Moore-Stiles farm, Lumberton Vic., Burlington County, New Jersey. William H. Kenderdine, delineator, 1937. P & P, HABS NJ-453; HABS, NJ, 3-LUMTO.V, 2-, sheet no. 1.

3-028

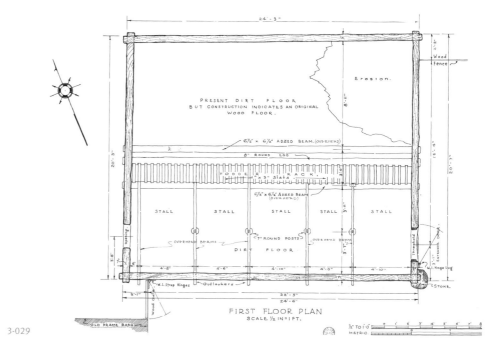

3-029

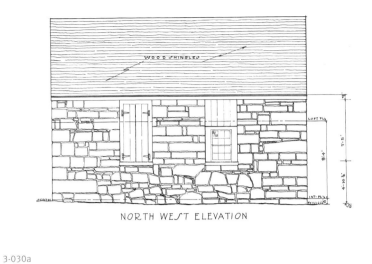

NORTH WEST ELEVATION

3-030a

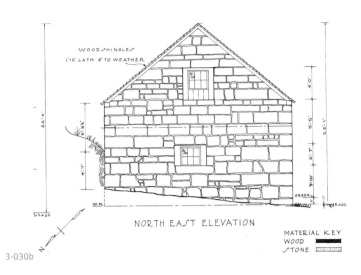

NORTH EAST ELEVATION

MATERIAL KEY
WOOD
STONE

3-030b

FIRST FLOOR PLAN

3-030c

3-030a. Northwest elevation of the Dennis stone barn, Johnsonburg, Warren County, New Jersey, ca. 1850. J. Caragol, delineator, 1937. P & P, HABS NJ-441; HABS, NJ, 21-JONBU, 2-, sheet no. 1, detail.

3-030b. Northeast elevation of the Dennis stone barn, Johnsonburg, Warren County, New Jersey, ca. 1850. J. Caragol, delineator, 1937. P & P, HABS NJ-441; HABS, NJ, 21-JONBU, 2-, sheet no. 1, detail.

3-030c. Floor plan of the Dennis stone barn, Johnsonburg, Warren County, New Jersey, ca. 1850. J. Caragol, delineator, 1937. P & P, HABS NJ-441; HABS, NJ, 21-JONBU, 2-, drawing no. 1, detail.

3-031. Abel Nicholson barn, Elsinboro, Salem County, New Jersey. George Neuschafer, photographer, 1941. P & P, HABS NJ-305; HABS, NJ, 17-HANBR.V, 3-A-1.

3-031

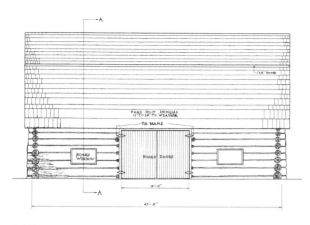

3-032

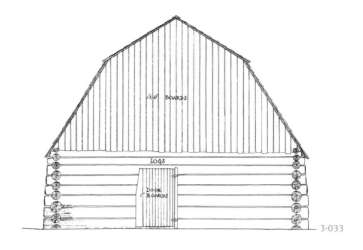

3-033

3-032. North elevation of Old Log Barn, Coudersport, Potter County, Pennsylvania, 1900. L. Nordstrom, V. Farrell, delineators, 1936. P & P, HABS PA-5127; HABS, PA, 53-____,1- , sheet no. 1.

While built in the twentieth century, this barn harkens back to the period of first settlement. After clearing a new piece of land, the farmer used the trees that were felled as logs for the walls of his barn. Using an older mode of log construction for the barn's base, he covered the building with a more up-to-date gambrel roof.

3-033. East elevation of Old Log Barn, Coudersport, Potter County, Pennsylvania, 1900. L. Nordstrom, V. Farrell, delineators, 1936. P & P, HABS PA-5127; HABS, PA, 53-____,1- , sheet no. 2.

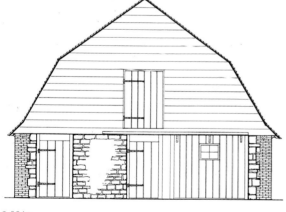

3-034a

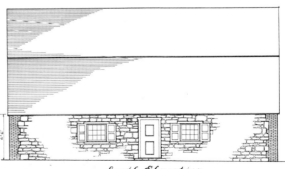

3-034b

3-034a. East elevation of the Old Barn, Germonds, Rockland County, New York. Frederick Jaeger, D. H. Ponty, delineators, 1937. P & P, HABS NY-6354; HABS, NY, 44-GERM, 1-, sheet no. 3, detail.

This building may be a house that was transformed into a barn by the removal of its internal partitions and the addition of two gable end doors. The south elevation (3-034b) has the window-door-window fenestration pattern of a house and a gambrel roof with a slight "kick" or flare at the eaves, more typical of houses.

3-034b. South elevation of the Old Barn, Germonds, Rockland County, New York. Frederick Jaeger, D. H. Ponty, delineators, 1937. P & P, HABS NY-6354; HABS, NY, 44-GERM, 1-, sheet no. 3, detail.

THREE-BAY BARNS

The three-bay barns in the Mid-Atlantic region are generally understood as a mark of English influence on local building design. Used to shelter livestock and their feed, one side was used to stable animals and the other side served as a haymow. Animals were fed by pitching the hay across the central passage, which could be used as a threshing floor at harvest time as well as a place to keep a wagon and other equipment.

3-035

3-035. Barn of Daniel Simpson, Jefferson County, New York. December, 1937. Arthur Rothstein, photographer. P & P, LC-USF34-026209-D.

3-036. Three-bay barn in the Finger Lakes Region, New York. October, 1941. John Collier, photographer. P & P, LC-USF34-81473-E.

3-036

3-037a. North elevation of the Retirement Barn, Biddles Corner Vic., New Castle County, Delaware, c. 1800. B. Herman, M. Fike, William Macintire, delineators, 1985. P & P, HABS DE-219; HABS, DE, 2-BIDCO.V,3-, sheet no. 1, detail.

3-037b. Floor plan of the Retirement Barn, Biddles Corner Vic., New Castle County, Delaware, c. 1800. B. Herman, M. Fike, William Macintire, delineators, 1985. P & P, HABS DE-219; HABS, DE, 2-BIDCO.V,3-, sheet no. 1, detail.

3-038a. South elevation, Horton-Wickham-Landon barn, Cutchogue, Suffolk County, New York. Carl B. Stove, delineator, 1940. P & P, HABS NY-5417; HABS, NY, 52-CUTHC, 1A-, sheet no. 1, detail.

Built to accompany a house constructed in 1649, this barn may be of similar vintage. Its corner posts (three for each bent in the main section of the barn), as indicated in the sectional view (3-038c), are hewn into a "gunstock" form so that their tops flare out and are considerably wider than the rest of the beam to make more wood available at the point where the plate, rafter, and girt have to be attached to the post. Hewing a gunstock post requires considerable effort because much of the tree must be cut away. Elaborate woodwork of this sort was much more common during the seventeenth century and its presence clearly indicates the antiquity of this barn.

3-038b. Plan of the Horton-Wickham-Landon barn, Cutchogue, Suffolk County, New York. Carl B. Stove, delineator, 1940. P & P, HABS NY-5417; HABS, NY, 52-CUTHC, 1A-, sheet no. 1, detail.

3-038c. Section of the Horton-Wickham-Landon barn, Cutchogue, Suffolk County, New York. Carl B. Stove, delineator, 1940. P & P, HABS NY-5417; HABS, NY, 52-CUTHC, 1A-, sheet no. 1, detail.

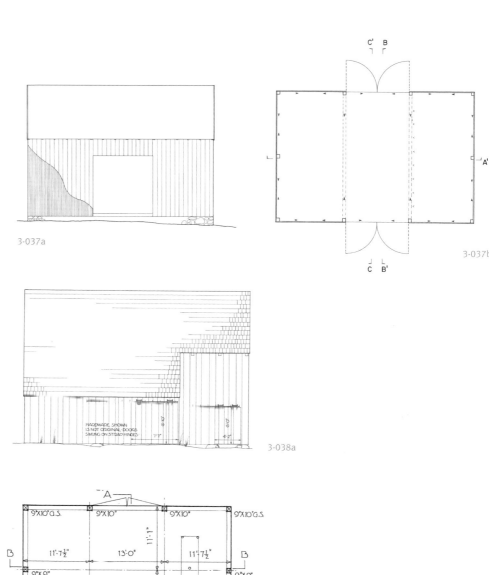

3-037a

3-037b

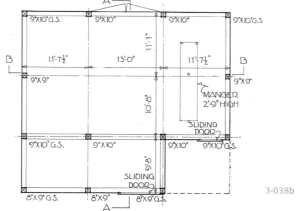

3-038a

3-038b

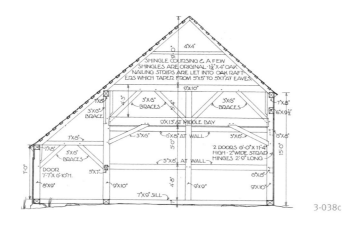

3-038c

3-039

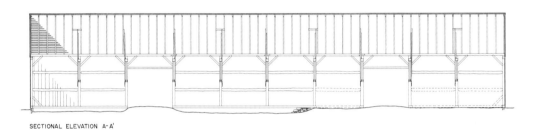

SECTIONAL ELEVATION A-A'

3-040

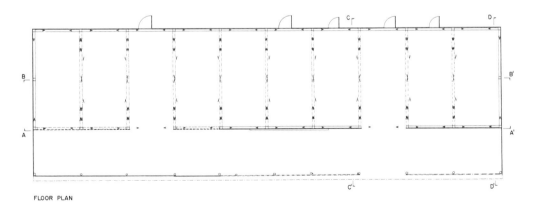

FLOOR PLAN

3-041

3-039. Old stone barn, Mountainville, Hunterdon County, New Jersey. Jack E. Boucher, photographer, 1972. P & P, HABS NJ-888; HABS, NJ, 10-MTVI, 2-1.

3-040. Sectional elevation of the Cochran Grange threshing barn, Middletown Vic., New Castle County, Delaware. Charles Bergengren, delineator, 1982. P & P, HABS DE-208-C; HABS, DEL, 2-MIDTO.V, 3-C, sheet no. 2, detail.

This drawing and fig. 3-041 reveal a design strategy available to a farmer operating in the three-bay tradition when he needed a larger barn. In the Cochran Grange barn the building is conceptually two five-bay barns built end to end. To develop this plan the builder simply expanded the three-bay plan by adding an extra bay at each end. While in theory he could have continued to add more bays, in practice such additions would have made the barn cumbersome because the end bays would be hard to reach from the central entrance. By doubling the single five-bay plan, no storage area is more than one bay from an entrance.

3-041. Floor plan of the Cochran Grange threshing barn, Middletown Vic., New Castle County, Delaware. Charles Bergengren, delineator, 1982. P & P, HABS DE-208-C; HABS, DEL, 2-MIDTO.V, 3-C-, sheet no. 1, detail.

3-042. South elevation of the Stone Barn Farm of John Black, Jr., Eayrestown Vic., Burlington County, New Jersey. Ernest L. Ergood, delineator, 1936. P & P, HABS NJ-254; HABS, NJ, 3-EARTO.V, 1-, sheet no. 2, detail.

Other ways to enlarge a three-bay barn involve the building of extensions. At the Stone Barn Farm, a substantial carriage house was added to the western end of the hay barn.

3-043. Thompson-Neely-Pedcock barn, Washington Crossing, Bucks County, Pennsylvania. Charles H. Dornbusch, photographer, 1941. P & P, HABS PA- 5203; HABS, PA, 9-WACRO.V, 1A-1.

Extra space in this barn was created by a adding a shed across the back of the building and a long shed off one corner which produces a barn with an L-shaped plan.

3-044. Hay barn near Elmira, New York. October, 1941. John Collier, photographer. P & P, LC-USF34-081213-C.

Here an L-shaped barn was created by joining two three-bay barns to a silo. This pattern provides both sections of the barn with direct access to the source of feed for the livestock as well as shelter from the prevailing north or west wind.

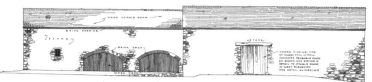

·SOUTH· ELEVATION·

3-042

3-043

3-044

TWO-LEVEL DAIRY BARNS

The two-level dairy barn made its appearance in New York about 1850 when the traditional practice of general cultivation was supplanted by a shift to dairy farming. Larger herds of milk cows required greater hay storage capacity, a demand that gave rise to a new barn type. In the newly invented two-level dairy barn, also known as a basement barn or raised three-bay barn, a standard three-bay barn stood upon a one-story masonry foundation. Frequently built on sloping land, this barn is essentially a type of bank barn with feed kept above the stock. The most distinctive feature of the design of this dairy barn is that in the upper level the central passage runs front to back while on the lower level the passage runs gable to gable. This biaxial configuration sets the barn apart from the celebrated bank barns of Pennsylvania. While the two-level dairy barn is concentrated most strongly in upstate New York, examples can be found throughout the Mid-Atlantic states (see, for example, 3-051 and 3-052) and elsewhere.

3-045

3-045. Dairy barn in the Catskill region, New York. June, 1943. John Collier, photographer. P & P, LC-USW3-34690-C.

3-046. Dairy barn along the upper Delaware River in New York. June, 1943. John Collier, photographer. P & P, LC-USW3-34700-C.

Occasionally the entrance to the upper section of a two-level dairy barn is protected by a short covered bridge. (A similar bridge can also be seen in 3-047).

3-047. Barn on the Daxater dairy farm near Little Falls, New York. October, 1941. John Collier, photographer. P & P, LC-USF34-081352-D.

3-048. Dairy barn, Hoyt Farm, Patterson, Putnam County, New York. Rob Tuchor, photographer, 1989. P & P, HABS NY-6300; HABS, NY, 40-PAT, 2-G-3.

The gable-end access to the basement-level stables at right is clearly visible in this image.

3-046

3-047

3-048

3-049

3-050

3-051

3-049. Dairy barn, Orange County, New York. November,1939. Arthur Rothstein, photographer. P & P, LC-USF34-003458-M1.

3-050. Dairy barn near Spencer, New York. September, 1940. Jack Delano, photographer. P & P, LC-USF34-41502-D.

3-051. Dairy barn, Tench Francis farm, Mantua Creek, Gloucester County, New Jersey, ca. 1770. Nathaniel R. Ewan, 1938. P & P, HABS NJ-410; HABS, NJ, 8-PABO.V, 2-5.

3-052. Dairy barn, John Turn Farm, Middle Smithfield, Monroe County, Pennsylvania. George A. Eisenman, photographer, 1970. P & P, HABS PA-1274; HABS, PA, 45-SHAWD.V, 7B-1.

PENNSYLVANIA LOG BARNS

The decision by the National Park Service to create a record of all the barns of Civil War vintage standing near the celebrated Gettysburg battlefield resulted in the thorough documentation of a community of old log barns. These buildings belong to a class of German barn known as *Grundscheier* or ground barn. Collectively these barns offer some clues to the development of the celebrated bank barns of Pennsylvania.

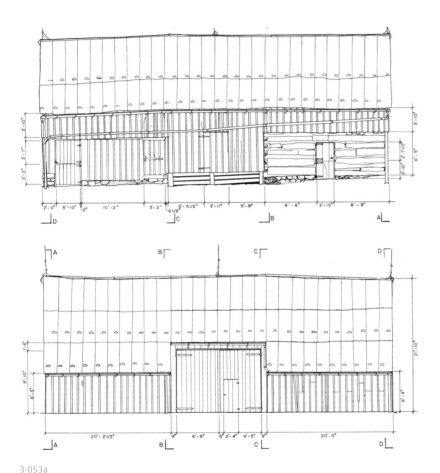

3-053a

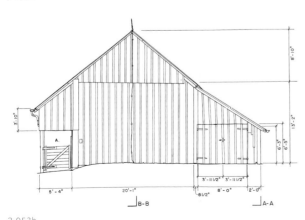

3-053b

3-053a. North and south elevations of the John Slyder barn, Gettysburg, Adams County, Pennsylvania, c. 1850. John S. Heisner, delineator, 1985. P & P, HABS PA-356-B; HABS, PA, 1-GET, 48- , sheet no. 3, detail.

The John Slyder barn can be viewed as a three-bay barn built with logs; it consists of two log pens that are separated by a central passage. The cribs are rather tall so that there is space for a lower level that serves as animal shelter, while the upper section provides an area for storing feed. There is a clear advantage to keeping hay above the animals' stalls; it allows them to be fed simply by dropping the hay through slots in the floor of the loft. In this barn we see that the upper section overhangs the lower level in the front with a projecting cantilevered forebay, one of the most distinctive features of a Pennsylvania bank barn (see 3-053b).

3-053b. West elevation of the John Slyder barn, Gettysburg, Adams County, Pennsylvania, c. 1850. John S. Heisner, delineator, 1985. P & P, HABS PA-356-B; HABS, PA, 1-GET, 48- , sheet no. 3, detail.

3-054. Southeast elevation of the George Weikert barn, Gettysburg, Adams County, Pennsylvania, ca. 1850. Wade Freitag, delineator, 1985. P & P, HABS PA-358; HABS, PA, 1-GET.V, 6B- , sheet no. 3.

The George Weikert barn was built initially as two-thirds of a *Grundscheier*. One crib and the passage were constructed with logs; at a later date the barn was given a balanced symmetrical appearance with the addition of a frame crib to its eastern end. When extended to its current length, a pent roof was erected over the stable entrances on the front of the barn (see 3-056).

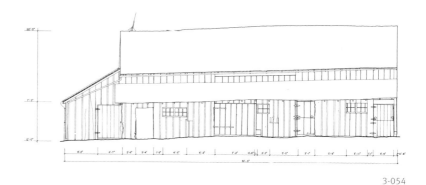

3-054

3-055. Framing elevation of the George Weikert barn, Gettysburg, Adams County, Pennsylvania, ca. 1850. Wade Freitag, delineator, 1985. P & P, HABS PA-358; HABS, PA, 1-GET.V, 6B- , sheet no. 4.

3-056. Floor plan of the George Weikert barn, Gettysburg, Adams County, Pennsylvania, ca. 1850. Allan E. Stockler, delineator, 1985. P & P, HABS PA-358; HABS, PA, 1-GET.V, 6B- , sheet no. 2.

In the plan the pent roof is indicated by the dashed line extending along the bottom of the drawing, which shows how the forebay overhangs the front of the barn.

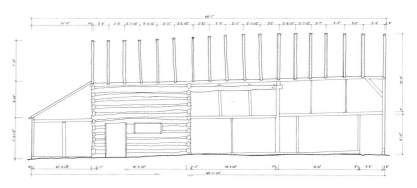

3-055

3-057. East elevation of the Bushman barn, Gettysburg, Adams County, Pennsylvania, 1808. Anthony W. Hron, delineator, 1985. P & P, HABS PA-365-A; HABS, PA, 1-GET, 8-A- , sheet no. 4.

The Bushman barn is five bays long and consists of two log cribs, one frame crib, and two passages. It appears that when the initial log *Grundscheier* proved to be too small, a frame extension was appended to the northern end with enough space to allow for the creation of a second entry (see 3-058). The expansion from a single- to a double-entry barn anticipates the design of the larger Pennsylvania bank barns, which may be over 100 feet long and equipped with multiple entries (see 3-066 for an example).

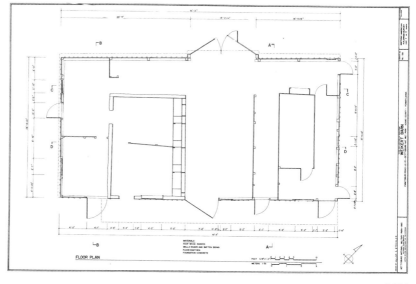

3-056

3-058. Framing elevation for the Bushman barn, Gettysburg, Adams County, Pennsylvania, 1808. Anthony W. Hron, delineator, 1985. P & P, HABS PA-365-A; HABS, PA, 1-GET, 8-A- , sheet no. 6.

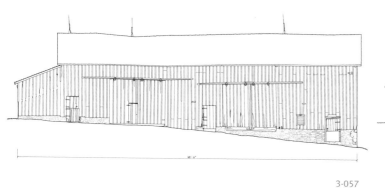

3-057

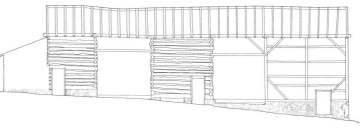

3-058

BANK BARNS
Cantilevered Forebay Barns

Of all the major types of the Pennsylvania bank barn, examples with cantilevered forebays are the most visually impressive. The forebay consists of the portion of the upper level of the barn that extends over the foundation, supported only by the strength of the floor joists. The forebay may extend out from the barn as much as 6 to 8 feet. Its purpose is to shelter the entrances of the stables or milking stalls from the weather as well as to provide additional storage or work space on the upper level. If the barn is built of stone or brick, the forebay is a framed structure that is tied to the internal framing of the barn (3-059–3-062, 3-065a). If the upper level is a frame or log structure, the forebay consists of that portion that extends past the front wall of the semi-subterranean foundation (3-005, 3-063).

Recent scholarship has shown that the Pennsylvania bank barn, once believed to be a locally invented form, has several important European antecedents. Most important are barns with deep overhanging forebays found in the borderlands of Switzerland and Austria. In Pennsylvania-German dialect bank barns with cantilevered forebays are known as *Schweiser Scheier;* that is, Swiss barns. While some bank barns probably emerged from an amalgam of influences, the majority began as Swiss imports.

3-059

3-059. Hopewell Furnace bank barn, Hopewell, Berks County, Pennsylvania. Photographer unknown, ca. 1960. P & P, HABS PA-5166; HABS, PA, 6-HOPVI, 16-1.

3-060. Dundore Farm barn, Mt. Pleasant, Berks County, Pennsylvania. Anthony Bley, photographer, 1975. P & P, HABS PA-261-A; HABS, PA, 6-MTPLES.V, 7B-2.

3-061. John H. Schriner barn, Lititz, Lancaster County, Pennsylvania, 1827. Charles H. Dornbusch, photographer, 1941. P & P, HABS PA-5226; HABS, PA, 36-LIT, 1A-1.

3-062. North elevation and section of the Trostle barn, Gettysburg, Adams County, Pennsylvania, early nineteenth century. Marla J. Felber, delineator, 1985. P & P, HABS PA-1962; HABS, PA, 1-GET.V, 17A- , sheet no. 8.

3-063. Bank barn, Farmville, Lancaster County, Pennsylvania. Charles H. Dornbusch, photographer, 1941. P & P, HABS PA-5209; HABS, PA,36-FARM.V, 1A-2.

3-060

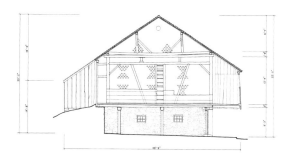

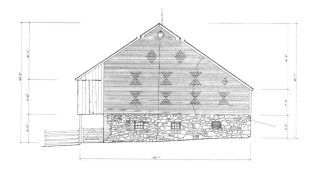

3-062

3-061

3-063

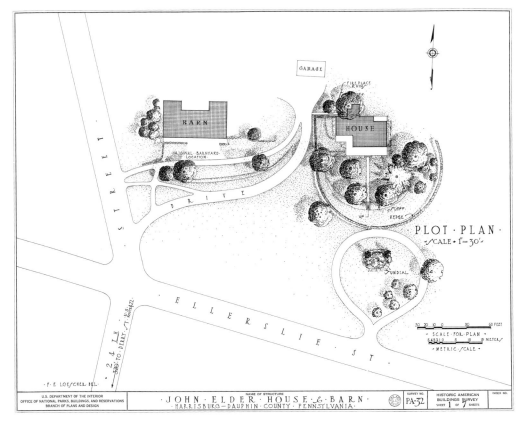

3-064

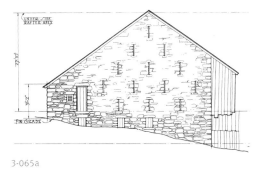

3-065a

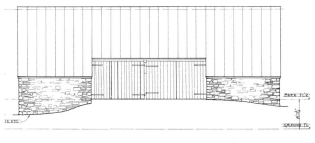

3-065b

3-066

3-064. John Elder house and barn, Paxtang, Dauphin County, Pennsylvania. F. E. Loescher, delineator, 1935. P & P, HABS PA-32; HABS, PA, 22-PAX, 2-, sheet no. 1.

The site plan for the John Elder house and barn reveals that the two are arranged with the ridge lines of their roofs closely aligned. The resulting visual link suggests that old medieval designs in which the house and barn were connected as one single building might have been lurking in the minds of some Pennsylvania farmers.

3-065a. West elevation of the John Elder barn, Paxtang, Dauphin County, Pennsylvania. F. E. Loescher, delineator, 1935. P & P, HABS PA-32; HABS, PA, 22-PAX, 2-, sheet no. 7, detail.

3-065b. North elevation of the John Elder barn, Paxtang, Dauphin County, Pennsylvania. F. E. Loescher, delineator, 1935. P & P, HABS PA-32; HABS, PA, 22-PAX, 2-, sheet no. 7, detail.

3-066. Bank barn, Mechanicsville, Lancaster County, Pennsylvania. Charles H. Dornbusch, photographer, 1941. P & P, HABS PA-5208; HABS, PA, 36-MECH.V, 1A-1.

This barn has three doors into its upper level. These doors open onto areas that are used to store farm machinery and, in season, to thresh grain.

Post-Supported Forebay Barns

Bank barns with forebays supported by posts or pillars fall into two categories. Those barns with only a modest overhang are referred to as "posted standard forebay barns" (see 3-067–3-070). If the forebay reaches out 15 feet or more and serves as an extra, separate storage room, usually for straw, the barn is called an "extended supported forebay barn" (see 3-071–3-076). However, in some locales such a barn might be called a "porch barn."

3-067

3-067. High Farm, Pipersville, Bucks County, Pennsylvania. Jack E. Boucher, photographer, 1990. P & P, HABS PA-5591-C; HABS, PA, 9-PIPERV, 1C-3.

3-068

3-069

3-070

3-068. Bank barn, Bacton Vic., Chester County, Pennsylvania. Charles H. Dornbusch, photographer, 1941. P & P, HABS PA-5243; HABS, PA,15-BACT.V, 2A-1.

3-069. Yoder barn, Lobachsville, Berks County, Pennsylvania. Cervin Robinson, photographer, 1958. P & P, HABS PA-1060; HABS, PA,6-LOBA.V, 1B-1.

Here the extensions to the barn are appended to both the forebay and the ramp sides.

3-070. John Romans barn, Romansville, Chester County, Pennsylvania. Ned Goode, photographer, 1959. P & P, HABS PA-165; HABS, PA, 15-ROMAV, 24-2.

The forebays for this barn, and the two in figs. 3-073 and 3-074, are supported by conical columns of stone masonry. These stone columns are found widely in Chester County, Pennsylvania, and their use is attributed to English Quakers who were adding large forebays to their English-style bank barns.

3-071. Graeme Park barn, Montgomery County, Pennsylvania. Cervin Robinson, photographer, 1958. P & P, HABS PA-579-A; HABS, PA, 46-HORM, 1A-1.

3-072. Bank barn, Charlestown Vic., Chester County, Pennsylvania. Charles H. Dornbusch, photographer, 1941. P & P, HABS PA-5242; HABS, PA, 15-CHAST.V, 1A-2.

The ambitious extended forebay here wraps around the gable end of the barn.

3-073. Southwest elevation, Couper bank barn, Tybouts Corner, New Castle County, Delaware. Charles Bergengren, William Macintire, delineators, 1982. P & P, HBS DE-217; HABS, DEL, 2-TYCO.V, 2-, sheet no. 3.

This barn is a three-level barn, sometimes called a "double-decker," with a granary and hay store above the stable. The wide space between the bank and the ramp side entrance to the second level was provided to allow wagons easy access to the granary floor (see 3-083).

3-074. Section, Couper bank barn, Tybouts Corner, New Castle County, Delaware. Charles Bergengren, William Macintire, delineators, 1982. P & P, HABS DE-217; HABS, DEL, 2-TYCO.V, 2-, sheet no. 4.

3-071

3-072

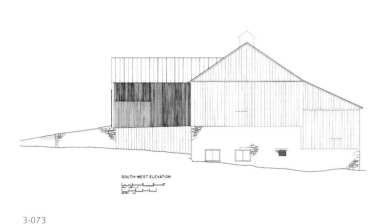

SOUTH-WEST ELEVATION

3-073

SECTION A-A'

3-074

End Wall–supported Forebay Barns

Bank barns that have their forebays supported by the extension of the gable-end walls (also known as "closed forebay barns" because the sides of the forebay are enclosed on the ground level) have been explained, in part, by the declining supply of timbers large enough to support a large cantilevered forebay. When the sill beam of the forebay was anchored to the thick stone end walls, the forebay received a measure of support. However, the floor joists that extend beyond the front wall of the stable are below the sill beam and thus provide most of the support for the forebay. A more compelling explanation for the rise of the end wall–supported forebay barn is found in aesthetic decisions. Over time Pennsylvania farmers discovered that the closed forebay not only provided an overhang that usefully protected the stable entrances but also gave them a barn with a balanced, symmetrical profile.

3-075. Decorated barn, Pricetown, Berks County, Pennsylvania. Charles H. Dornbusch, photographer, 1941. P & P, HABS PA-5269; HABS, PA, 6-PRICE, 1A-1.

3-076. Decorated barn, Montgomery County, Pennsylvania. Charles H. Dornbusch, photographer, 1941. P & P, HABS PA-5349; HABS, PA, 46- ____, 7-1.

3-075

3-076

3-077

3-078

3-079

3-080

3-077. Barn, East Texas Vic., Lehigh County, Pennsylvania. Charles H. Dornbusch, photographer, 1941. P & P, HABS PA-5308; HABS, PA, 39-ETEX.V, 1A-1.

3-078. Decorated barn, Center Valley, Lehigh County, Pennsylvania. Charles H. Dornbusch, photographer, 1941. P & P, HABS PA-5321; HABS, PA, 39-CENVA, 1A-1.

3-079. Barn, East Texas Vic., Lehigh County, Pennsylvania. Charles H. Dornbusch, photographer, 1941. P & P, HABS PA-5307; HABS, PA, 39-ETEX.V, 2A-1.

3-080. Kaufman barns, Oley, Berks County, Pennsylvania. Ned Goode, photographer, 1958. P & P, HABS PA-1059; HABS, PA, 6-OLEY.V, 1B-1.

3-081. John Jacobs barn, Bacton, Chester County, Pennsylvania. Ned Goode, photographer, 1958. P & P, HABS PA-1209A ; HABS, PA, 15-BACT, 1A-1.

3-081

Stone-arched Forebay Barns

The stone-arched forebay barn is a subtype of the closed forebay barn. The decision to build the front wall of the barn in stone rather than wood requires the use of substantial arches in order to support the weight of the wall and still allow access to the stables.

3-082

3-083

3-082. Lukens stone barn, Barren Hill, Montgomery County, Pennsylvania. Charles H. Dornbusch, photographer, 1941. P & P, HABS PA-5255; HABS, PA, 46-BARRHI, 1A-1.

3-083. Lowndes Taylor barn, West Chester Vic., Chester County, Pennsylvania. Ned Goode, 1958. P & P, HABS PA-1100; HABS, PA, 15-WCHES.V, 1-1.

Like the Couper bank barn from Delaware (3-073), this barn has three levels, as indicated by the two tiers of openings in the forebay wall. Also note the two ramp levels visible at the left edge of the photograph.

ENGLISH BANK BARNS

English bank barns that lack the distinctive forebay can be traced to the so-called Lake District of northwestern England. In that hilly region the usual three-bay barn was built on sloping ground above a basement stable for animals. In the place of an overhanging forebay the entrances to the stables were protected by a long pent roof. Barns of this type are found in Pennsylvania mainly in the counties near Philadelphia, which had a large number of English settlers.

3-084

3-084. William Miller barn, Avondale, Chester County, Pennsylvania. Ned Goode, photographer, 1958. P & P, HABS PA-5137-A; HABS, PA, 15-AVON, 1A-1.

While the pent roof has been lost, the flashing line and beam stumps indicate its former presence across the front and gable end of the barn.

3-085

3-085. Witherspoon barn, Princeton, Mercer County, New Jersey. Jack E. Boucher, photographer, 1964. P & P, HABS NJ-801; HABS, NJ, 11-PRINT, 22-2.

3-086. Southwest view of barn, Corner Ketch, New Castle County, Delaware. David Ames, photographer, 1983. P & P, HABS DE-205; HABS, DEL, 2-CORNK.V, 3-1.

Built around 1800, this English bank barn was modified extensively in the late nineteenth century by the addition of a large shed to its eastern gable (this view shows the north and east elevations). The extra space functioned like a forebay, providing additional room for the storage of straw and hay at a time when the farm owner was expanding his dairy production.

3-087. Northeast view of barn, Corner Ketch, New Castle County, Delaware. David Ames, photographer, 1983. P & P, HABS DE-205; HABS, DEL, 2-CORNK.V, 3-2.

3-086

3-087

The national trend for building round barns produced a few Mid-Atlantic examples, but interestingly some of them show the influence of the bank barn tradition by being built into a hill with their stables on the lower level.

The designs for this selection of Mid-A
tional to the extraordinarily decorative
wagons on the ground floor while hay
these structures were rarely decorate
because the stables that are attached
ted in a wide range of decorative feat
ers (3-100–3-101).

3-092. Stable in Delhi, New York. June, 1943
photographer. P & P, LC-USW3-34706-C.

3-093. Elevation and floor plan of the Denni
wagon shed, Johnsonburg, Warren County, I
G. Kilgus, delineator, 1937. P & P, HABS NJ-
JONBU, 2-, sheet no. 2.

The two sheds to the right are appended to
serves as a stable and general storage spa
3-030c for drawings of the barn).

3-088. Sheely farm in Adams County, Pennsylvania. Sheldon Dick, photographer, 1938. P & P, LC-USF34-040073-D.

3-089. Wylie-Miller barn, Washington Vic., Washington County, Pennsylvania, 1888. Edward Bonfilo, Antoni de Chicchis, delineators, 1962. P & P, HABS PA-427; HABS, PA, 63-WASH.V, 1- , drawing no. 5.

3-088

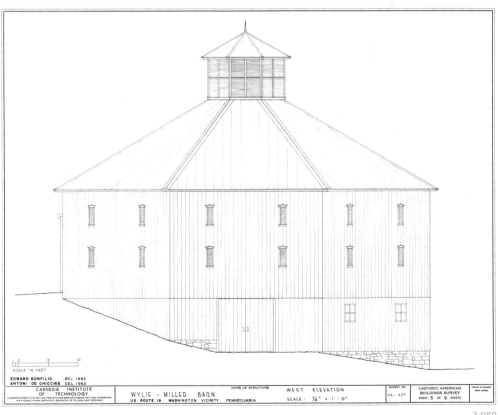

3-089

HOPS BARNS

Hops were introduced as a cash c
tinued until the coming of Prohib
hops (actually the cones produce
stored and processed for shippir
roof. Two stories tall, it was lined
second level was a grill-like arra
tles of brimstone would rise up
be ventilated through a chimne

3-098

3-090

3-091

3-099

3-100

3-101

3-098. Burholme stables, Philadelphia, Philadelphia County, Pennsylvania. Jack E. Boucher, photographer, 1972. P & P, HABS PA-186-A; HABS, PA, 51-PHILA, 273A-1.

3-099. Harry Endsley stable, Johnstown, Cambria County, Pennsylvania. Jet Lowe, photographer, 1988. P & P, HABS PA-5732-B; HABS, PA, 11-JOTO, 84-B-1.

3-100. Bowman's Castle stable, Brownsville, Fayette County, Pennsylvania. Jack E. Boucher, photographer, 1963. P & P, HABS PA-429-A; HABS, PA, 26-BROVI, 1A-1.

3-101. Georgian Court stable, Lakewood, New Jersey. William Henry Jackson, photographer, 1900. P & P, DPCC, LC-D4-13380.

Built in 1898 for millionaire George Jay Gould, Georgian Court was a vast estate, much of it devoted to gardens patterned after the grounds of the palace of Louis XIV at Versailles. The stable, which provided shelter for Gould's polo ponies, was topped by a tall steeple that served as a support for the stable's water tank.

OUTBUILDINGS

Hay Barracks, Corncribs, Granaries, and Chicken Houses

The hay barrack was an open-sided structure intended to provide a roof over a haystack. The Dutch are to be credited for bringing the barrack, widely known in Europe, to North America. Once a common sight in the Hudson Valley, farmers in New England and Pennsylvania also built hay barracks. Usually the support poles, which were drilled with holes at regular intervals, extended through the roof. Because the roof only rested on a set of removable wooden pegs, it could then be raised or lowered to accommodate the height of the stack with the aid of a ratcheting jack. The support pegs were then replaced at the required level. But at the Mondamon Farm (3-102) the roof was solidly attached to the top of its poles.

3-105a.
Bergen (
HABS N,

The De (
were dri
of bins \
whole s
keep ou

3-105b.
Bergen
HABS N

3-105c.
Bergen
HABS N

3-102. Mondamon Farm hay barrack, Biddles Corner Vic., New Castle County, Delaware. David Ames, photographer, 1982. P & P, HABS DE-225; HABS, DEL, 2-BIDCO.V, 2-1.

3-102

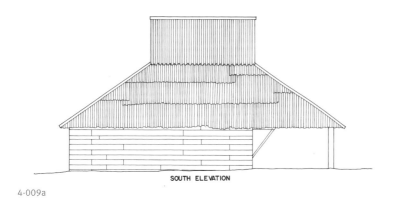

4-009a

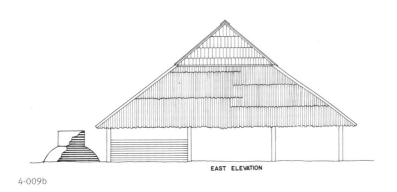

4-009b

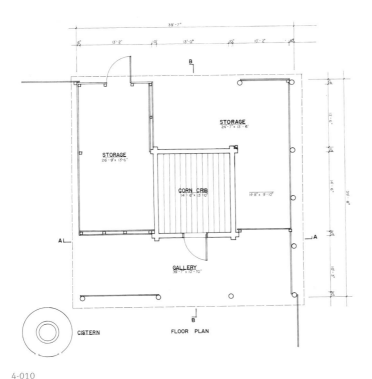

4-010

4-009a. South elevation, Oakland Plantation barn, Bermuda, Natchitoches Parish, Louisiana, ca. 1820. Rick Ward, delineator, 1987. P & P, HABS LA-1192-J; HABS, LA, 35-BERM, 2-J-, sheet no. 2, detail.

At the center of this barn stands a two-story corncrib (see 4-010). The sheds attached to all four sides of this log crib served as storage for feed and equipment associated with livestock.

4-009b. East elevation, Oakland Plantation barn, Bermuda, Natchitoches Parish, Louisiana. Rick Ward, delineator, 1987. P & P, HABS LA-1192-J; HABS, LA, 35-BERM, 2-J-, sheet no. 2, detail.

4-010. Plan, Oakland Plantation barn, Bermuda, Natchitoches Parish, Louisiana. Rick Ward, delineator, 1987. P & P, HABS LA-1192-J; HABS, LA, 35-BERM, 2-J-, sheet no. 1, detail.

Access to an underground cistern filled with rainwater collected off the roof of the barn is shown at the southeastern corner of the building. There were several cisterns on the plantation to provide an adequate supply of drinking water.

4-011. Barn at the Irwindale Farms, Georgia. June, 1936. Carl Mydans, photographer. P & P, LC-USF34-006707-D.

4-012. Loading hay at the Marcella Plantation, Mileston, Mississippi. November, 1939. Marion Post Wolcott, photographer. LC-USF34-052303-D.

4-013. Old barn in Mitchell County, Georgia. Photographer unknown, 1935. P & P, S-19934.

4-011

4-012

4-013

4-014

4-015

4-016

4-014. Barn, Bagatelle Plantation, Iberville Parish, Louisiana. A. C. Eschete, photographer, 1977. P & P, HABS LA-1142-D; HABS, LA, 47-____, 1D-1.

4-015. Barn at the H. M. Hendersen Farm, Ocilla, Georgia. Howard Wight Marshall, photographer, 1977. AFC, Survey of the Georgia Wire Grass Region, Ga. 4-17618, no. 20.

4-016. "Trinity" barn, Melrose, Natchitoches Parish, Louisiana. June, 1940. Marion Post Wolcott, photographer. P & P, LC-USF34-054645-D.

The tall central crib in this barn stands well above the two flanking sheds. This variation of a single-crib barn is called a "trinity" barn, a recognition of its three distinct sections.

4-017. Barn near Summerton, South Carolina. June, 1939. Marion Post Wolcott, photographer. P & P, LC-USF34-51941-D.

A form marking the impact of England traditions, three-bay barns have persisted in the lowland South for three centuries (4-018). These barns, when constructed in durable materials and impressive scale, could be quite striking (see 4-019). However, most were modest, in keeping with the prevailing regional ethic that favored expediency. The simple structure could be used to either store equipment or shelter livestock (4-020). With the rise of the citrus industry in Florida at the beginning of the twentieth century, the three-bay barn was enlisted as the barn of choice (4-021), proving once again the flexibility and utility of the structure.

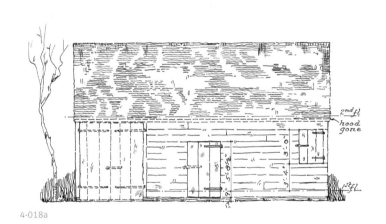

4-018a

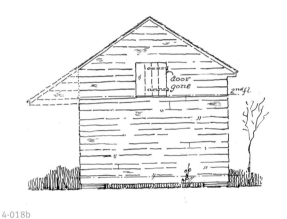

4-018b

4-018a. West elevation, Indian Range barn, McDaniel Vic., Talbot County, Maryland. Henry Chandlee Forman, delineator, 1962. P & P, HABS, MD-310; HABS, MD,21-MCDAN.V, 1-, sheet no. 1, detail.

4-018b. South elevation, Indian Range barn, McDaniel Vic., Talbot County, Maryland. Henry Chandlee Forman, delineator, 1962. P & P, HABS, MD-310; HABS, MD,21-MCDAN.V, 1-, sheet no. 1, detail.

4-018c. Plan, Indian Range barn, McDaniel Vic., Talbot County, Maryland. Henry Chandlee Forman, delineator, 1962. P & P, HABS, MD-310; HABS, MD,21-MCDAN.V, 1-, sheet no. 1, detail.

4-018c

· FIRST FLOOR PLAN ·

4-019. Linden barn, Baltimore Vic., Baltimore County, Maryland. E. H. Pickering, photographer, 1937. P & P, HABS, MD-848; HABS, MD, 3-____, 3-3.

4-020. Barn, Pleasant Farm, Beaufort, South Carolina. Photographer unknown. P & P, LC-USZ62-58575.

4-021. Barn, Orange Groves on Lake Concord, Orlando, Florida, 1900–1910. Photographer unknown. P & P, DPCC, LC-D4-33527.

4-019

4-020

4-021

TRANSVERSE-CRIB BARNS

The transverse-crib barn has its origins in the upland South, most likely near the headwaters of the Holston River sometime during the first quarter of the nineteenth century (5-
037–5-056). Eventually becoming the most popular barn type in the United States,
it understandably found its way onto the coastal plain of the lowland South. In plan the
building has its entrance in the gable end, which opens to a long central passage. Stables
were arranged on either side of this passage and hay was stored in the loft overhead.

4-022

4-022. Barn, Santa Maria Plantation, Baton Rouge, Louisiana. David J. Kaminsky, photographer, 1978. P & P, HABS, LA-1137; HABS, LA, 17-BATRO, 11-18.

4-023. Nolan Pettway's barn, Gee's Bend, Alabama. May, 1939. Marion Post Wolcott, photographer. P & P, LC-USF33-30361-M5.

4-024. Barn in Pike County, Alabama. March, 1939. Marion Post Wolcott, photographer. P & P, LC-USF34-051341.

Here a second passage runs along the side of the barn. Such additions to the symmetrical central-passage barn were usually constructed as attached sheds but here the roof reaches out to cover both the barn and its shed.

4-023

4-024

Plantation Barns

While there is no barn type that is exclusively linked to the plantation context, plantation barns are consistently among the region's most elaborate agricultural structures.

4-042

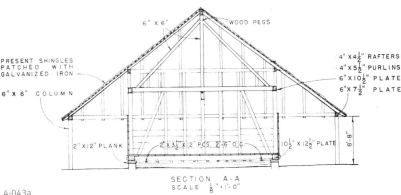

4-043a

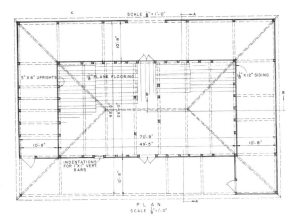

4-043b

4-042. Barn, Homeplace Plantation, Hahnville, St. Charles Parish, Louisiana. Lester Jones, photographer, 1940. P & P, HABS, LA-155; HABS, LA, 45-HAHNV, 1-15.

The barn at the Homeplace Plantation reveals its French cultural connections with its distinctive hipped roof. Its wide eaves extend well past the walls on all sides to provide shelter for animal stables on the sides and back of the barn. The front eaves serve as a deep gallery (see 4-043b).

4-043a. Section of the barn, Homeplace Plantation, Hahnville, St. Charles Parish, Louisiana. Adolph H. Felder, delineator, 1940. P & P, HABS, LA-155; HABS, LA, 45-HAHNV, 1-, sheet no. 10, detail.

The sectional view reveals a distinctive French mode of framing: there are two sets of rafters. The principal rafters stabilize the center king post (which supports the ridgepole at the apex of the roof) and the common rafters provide support for the sheathing and shingles that cover the roof.

4-043b. Plan of the barn, Homeplace Plantation, Hahnville, St. Charles Parish, Louisiana. Adolph H. Felder, delineator, 1940. P & P, HABS, LA-155; HABS, LA, 45-HAHNV, 1-, sheet no. 10, detail.

The plan reveals that at the center of this barn there stands a three-bay barn. Compare with the barn at Oakland Plantation near Natchitoches, Louisiana, which is a corncrib surrounded by sheds (4-009 and 4-010).

4-044. Barn, Hamilton Plantation, St. Simons Island, Georgia. Lawrence Bradley, photographer, 1936. P & P, HABS GA-219; HABS, GA, 64-SASI, 3-2.

This barn is constructed with tiers of a primitive type of concrete called "tabby" composed of sand, lime created by burning oyster shells, and whole oyster shells that serve as the aggregate. Initially used in the construction of seventeenth-century forts, the technique was rediscovered during the nineteenth century by Georgia planter Thomas Spalding and was widely used for antebellum plantation buildings constructed on the coastal islands near Brunswick.

4-045. Cotton gin and press barn, Magnolia Plantation, Natchitoches Vic., Natchitoches Parish, Louisiana. Christopher H. Marston, delineator, 1997. P & P, HAER, LA-11; HAER, LA, 35-NATCH.V, 3- , sheet no. 1, detail.

A leading plantation in the Cane River area, Magnolia had a factory-scale operation on its grounds. Planters usually sent their cotton fiber to a nearby town where it was ginned and pressed into bales. But the owners of Magnolia were ambitious enough to take on the expense of developing their own gin stand. Thus they were able not only to process their fiber but the fiber grown on all the neighboring plantations, a service for which they of course charged a substantial fee.

4-046. Longitudinal and transverse sections and plan of the cotton gin and press barn, Magnolia Plantation, Natchitoches Vic., Natchitoches Parish, Louisiana. Christopher H. Marston, Thomas Behrens, delineators, 1997. P & P, HAER, LA-11; HAER,LA, 35-NATCH.V, 3- , drawing no. 2.

In the longitudinal section the older type of cotton press that was turned by a team of mules walking around in a circle is seen to the left and the gin and press run by a steam engine is located on the right-hand side.

4-044

4-045

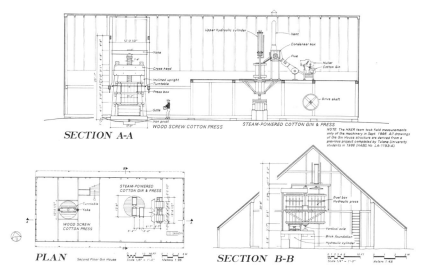

4-046

Stables

Horses were a powerful marker of personal status in the antebellum South. It was widely said that a man was "only as good as his horse." Consequently, special measures were taken to ensure that one's mount was always in the best condition. The usual regimen included the construction of special buildings reserved for horses set apart from the barn and other sheds. Given the importance of horses in the Old South, it is not surprising that the stables and carriage houses were usually the largest agricultural structures (see 4-053, 4-057, 4-062, and 4-063) on an estate, if not the most lavishly decorated of all farm buildings (4-058–4-061, 4-064).

4-047

4-048

4-047. Mule barn near Zebulon, North Carolina. March, 1942. Arthur Rothstein, photographer. P & P, LC-USW 3-452-D.

This stable and the next two examples (4-048 and 4-049) were located on small farms. Their modesty contrasts markedly with the other examples that stand on plantations or are connected to the homes of wealthy merchants.

4-048. Mule barn near Lakeview, Arkansas. December, 1938. Russell Lee, photographer. P & P, LC-USF34-31865-D.

4-049. Stable, Bowling Heights, Upper Marlboro, Prince George's County, Maryland. Jack E. Boucher, photographer, 1990. P & P, MD-964-D; HABS, MD, 17-MARBU, 8D-1.

4-049

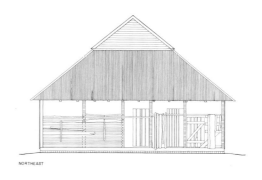

NORTHEAST

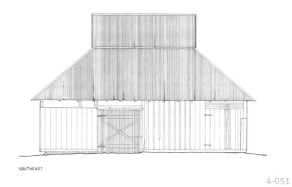

SOUTHEAST

4-051

4-050

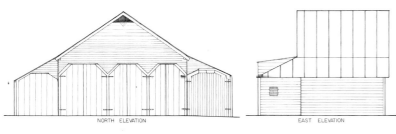

NORTH ELEVATION   EAST ELEVATION

4-052

4-053

4-050. Mule barn, Irwin County, Georgia. David Stanley, photographer, 1977. AFC, Survey of the Georgia Wire Grass Region, Ga. 4-17410, no. 34.

4-051. Northeast and southeast elevations of the stable, Oakland Plantation, Bermuda, Natchitoches Parish, Louisiana. Jeffery M. Solak, delineator, 1987. P & P, HABS-LA-1192-H; HABS, LA, 35-BER, 2-H-, sheet no. 2, detail.

This stable was initially a smokehouse that was modified by the addition of four sheds. The design of this building parallels the design of the plantation's barn (see 4-009 4-010).

4-052. North and east elevations of the carriage house, Oakland Plantation, Bermuda, Natchitoches Parish, Louisiana. James T. Murphy, delineator, 1987. P & P, HABS-1192-L; HABS, LA,35-BER, 2-L-, drawing no. 1.

4-053. Stable, Stratford Hall, Westmoreland County, Virginia. Theodor Horydczak, photographer, ca. 1925. P & P, Theodor Horydczak Collection, LC-H814-T-2374-048.

4-060

4-060. Stable, Uncle Sam Plantation, St. James Parish, Louisiana. Richard Koch, photographer, 1936. P & P, HABS, LA-74; HABS, LA, 47-CONV.V, 1-28.

4-061. Stable, Melrose, Natchez, Adams County, Mississippi. Jack E. Boucher, photographer, 1992. P & P, HABS, MS-61-L; HABS, MISS, 1-NATCH.V, 12L-2.

4-062. Carriage house, Melrose, Natchez, Adams County, Mississippi. Jack E. Boucher, photographer, 1992. P & P, HABS, MS-61-M; HABS, MISS, 1-NATCH.V, 12M-1.

4-061

4-062

4-063. Stable, Elmwood Plantation, Jefferson Parish, Louisiana. Frances Benjamin Johnston, photographer, 1938. P & P, LC-J7-LA-1229.

Built into the decorated central gable of this barn was a set of nesting boxes for pigeons. Compare this dovecote with those at other southern plantations (4-084–4-087).

4-064. Stable, Thomas Vowell house, Alexandria, Fairfax County, Virginia. Jack E. Boucher, photographer, 1972. P & P, HABS, VA-711; HABS,VA, 7-ALEX, 170A-1.

4-065. Stable, Benjamin Dulany house, Alexandria, Fairfax County, Virginia. Victor Amato, photographer, 1958. P & P, HABS, VA-447; HABS,VA, 7-ALEX, 65A-1.

4-063

4-064

4-065

4-066

4-066. Stable, Aiken-Rhett House, Charleston, Charleston County, South Carolina. Charles N. Bayless, photographer, 1979. P & P, HABS, SC-275; HABS, SC, 10-CHAR, 177B-1.

Built by Governor William Aiken, who owned one of the largest plantations in South Carolina, located on Jehosse Island, this stable stands on a large lot that extends the length of a city block. No building on his rural estate could have rivaled this stable except the rice mill, a huge shed that housed all the processing machinery.

Outbuildings

Because southern farming tradition required separate structures for each agricultural activity, farmyards typically contained an array of small buildings, including granaries, dovecotes, and chicken coops. Corncribs were important structures because of the central place of cornmeal in southern food ways. Not only is corn the universal grain in the South; even in the twenty-first century southern farmers produce a considerable share of the nation's corn crop. A corncrib was an obligatory building for a southern farm. Following several plans, some of them were only narrow boxes (4-069–4-071) and others were the size of a barn (4-074 and 4-075).

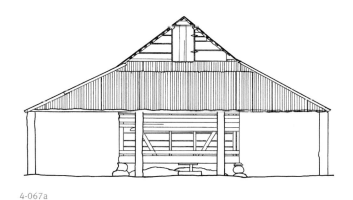

4-067a

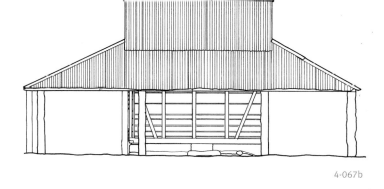

4-067b

4-067a. East elevation of the corncrib, Magnolia Plantation, Natchitoches Vic., Natchitoches Parish, Louisiana. Lister, delineator, 1987. P & P, HABS, LA-1193-G; HABS, LA, 35-NATCH.V, 2-G-, sheet no. 1, detail.

This corncrib has the same encircling sheds as the buildings at Oakland Plantation (see 4-009 and 4-051). Oakland and Magnolia Plantations were owned by the same family and stood on opposite banks of the Cane River.

4-067b. North elevation of the corncrib, Magnolia Plantation, Natchitoches Vic., Natchitoches Parish, Louisiana. Lister, delineator, 1987. P & P, HABS, LA-1193-G; HABS, LA, 35-NATCH.V, 2-G-, drawing no. 1.

4-067c. Plan of the corncrib, Magnolia Plantation, Natchitoches Vic., Natchitoches Parish, Louisiana. Lister, delineator, 1987. P & P, HABS, LA-1193-G; HABS, LA, 35-NATCH.V, 2-G-, sheet no. 1, detail.

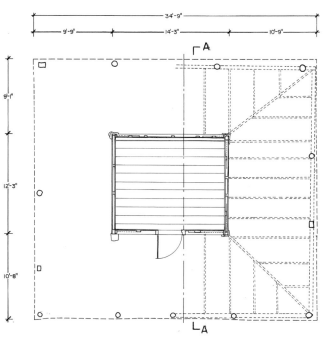

4-067c

4-068

4-068. Corncrib, Calvert Cliffs, Calvert County, Maryland. E. H. Pickering, photographer, 1936. P & P, HABS, MD-415; HABS, MD, 5-LUSB.V, 4-4.

4-069a. South elevation of the corncrib, Wye Town farm, Tunis Mills Vic., Talbot County, Maryland. Henry Chandlee Forman, delineator, 1962. P & P, HABS, MD-309; HABS, MD, 21-TUMI.V, 1- , sheet no. 1, detail.

4-069b. East elevation of the corncrib, Wye Town farm, Tunis Mills Vic., Talbot County, Maryland. Henry Chandlee Forman, delineator, 1962. P & P, HABS, MD-309; HABS, MD, 21-TUMI.V, 1- , sheet no. 1, detail.

4-069c. Floor plan of the corncrib, Wye Town farm, Tunis Mills Vic., Talbot County, Maryland. Henry Chandlee Forman, delineator, 1962. P & P, HABS, MD-309; HABS, MD, 21-TUMI.V, 1- , sheet no. 1, detail.

· SOUTH ELEVATION ·
(North similar)

4-069a

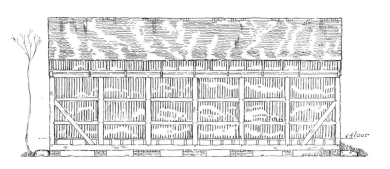

· EAST ELEVATION ·
(West similar except no raised eaves)

4-069b

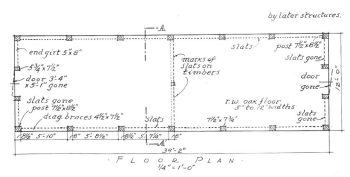

· FLOOR PLAN ·
1/4" = 1'-0"

4-069c

4-070

4-071

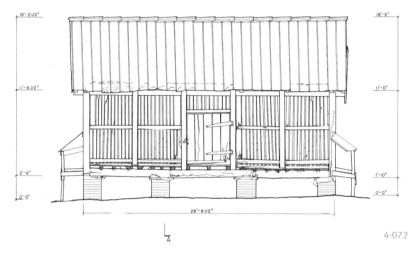

4-072

4-070. Corncrib, Day-Breedon farm, Calvert County, Maryland. Randolph Langenbach, photographer, 1973. P & P, HABS, MD-175-B; HABS, MD, 5-SOL.V, 2B-1.

4-071. Corncrib, Coffren house, Croom, Prince George's County, Maryland. Jack E. Boucher, photographer, 1990. P & P, HABS, MD-988-C; HABS, MD, 17-CROM, 2C-1.

4-072. Corncrib, Habre de Venture, La Plata Vic., Charles County, Maryland. Terry Bailey, delineator, 1985. P & P, HABS, MD-470-B; HABS, MD, 9-PORTO.V., 3B- , sheet no. 2, detail.

4-073. Corncrib, Belleview farm, Ft. Washington, Prince George's County, Maryland. Jack E. Boucher, photographer, 1989. P & P, HABS, MD-654-B; HABS, MD, 17-TIP.V, 2B-1.

4-073

4-074

4-075

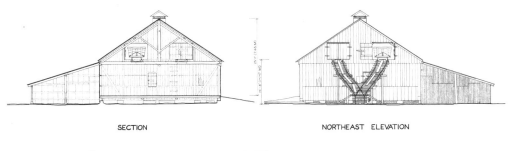
SECTION   NORTHEAST ELEVATION

SOUTHEAST ELEVATION

4-076

4-074. Corncrib, Wye house, Talbot County, Maryland. E. H. Pickering, photographer, 1936. P & P, HABS, MD-88-E; HABS, MD, 21-EATO.V, 2D-1.

4-075. Corncrib and stable, Mt. Lubentia, Prince George's County, Maryland. John Brostrup, photographer, 1936. P & P, HABS, MD-638-A; HABS, MD, 17-LARG.V, 1A-1.

The corncrib at Mt. Lubentia plantation was, at first, similar to corncribs seen at other plantations (compare it with 4-073), but it was expanded by the addition of a shed-roofed crib, which also created a protected drive-through.

4-076. Section and northeast and southeast elevations of the corncrib, Laurel Valley Sugar Plantation, Thibodaux, Lafourche Parish, Louisiana. John B. Murray, delineator, 1978. P & P, HAER-LA-1-D; HAER, LA, 29-THIB, 1D- , sheet no. 2.

This corncrib was designed by the Louden Company of Fairfield, Iowa. Intended to store the tons of grain needed to feed the 200 mules that pulled the plows and wagons on this vast sugar estate, a special trolley car mounted on tracks was used to carry harvested ears up into the upper level of the building (see section). When doors located along the base of the car were opened, some 3,000 pounds of corn cascaded down to the floor below.

In the sectional view the trolley car that was raised by a cable and winch into the loft is shown in the position from which its cargo would be emptied onto the floor below. The whole building was basically one large corn bin.

4-077. Granary, Northampton Plantation, Largo, Prince George's County, Maryland. John O. Brostrup, photographer, 1936. P & P, HABS, MD-639; HABS, MD, 17-LARG.V, 2-4.

4-078. Granary, Pleasant Hills, Prince George's County, Maryland. Jack E. Boucher, photographer, 1990. P & P, HABS, MD-1012-B; HABS, MD, 17-MARBU, 11B-1.

4-079. Granary near Amite, Louisiana. October, 1938. Russell Lee, photographer. P & P, LC-USF 33-11866-M1.

4-077

4-078

4-079

4-080

4-081

4-080. Dovecote, Bowman's Folly, Accomac Vic., Accomack County, Virginia. Jack E. Boucher, photographer, 1960. P & P, HABS, VA-634; HABS, VA, 1-AC.V, 1A-1.

The pigeons raised in this and the other dovecotes (4-081–4-087) were an element of the elegant meals enjoyed by a privileged planter's family. The status associated with these birds was signaled by the elaborate designs and decorations found on these buildings.

4-081. Dovecote, Hill Plantation, Washington Vic., Wilkes County, Georgia. Frances Benjamin Johnston, photographer, 1938. P & P, LC-J7-GA-1602.

4-082. Dovecote, Wingfield-Cade-Saunders House, Washington, Wilkes County, Georgia. Frances Benjamin Johnston, photographer, 1938. P & P, LC-J7-GA-1566.

4-083. Section, plan, and isometric view of the dovecote, Lakeside Plantation, Batchelor, Pointe Coupee Parish, Louisiana. Wanahmad Wanmaizan, delineator, 1987. P & P, HABS, LA-1180-A; HABS, LA, 39-BATCH, 1-A, sheet no. 2.

4-082

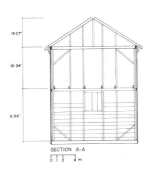

SECTION A-A

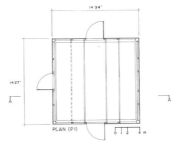

PLAN (P1)

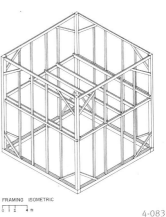

FRAMING ISOMETRIC

4-083

4-084

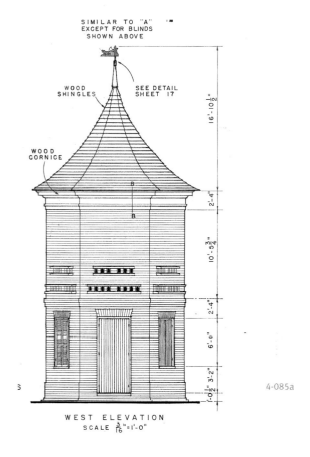

SIMILAR TO "A"
EXCEPT FOR BLINDS
SHOWN ABOVE

WOOD
SHINGLES

SEE DETAIL
SHEET 17

WOOD
CORNICE

WEST ELEVATION
SCALE 3/16"=1'-0"

4-085a

4-084. Dovecote, Uncle Sam Plantation, St. James Parish, Louisiana. Richard Koch, photographer, 1936. P & P, HABS, LA-74; HABS, LA, 47-CONV.V, 1-26.

4-085a. West elevation of the dovecote, Uncle Sam Plantation, St. James Parish, Louisiana. Adolph H. Felder, delineator, 1940. P & P, HABS, LA-74; HABS, LA, 47-CONV.V, 1- , sheet no. 14, detail.

4-085b. Floor plan of the dovecote, Uncle Sam Plantation, St. James Parish, Louisiana. Adolph H. Felder, delineator, 1940. P & P, HABS, LA-74; HABS, LA, 47-CONV.V, 1- , sheet no. 14, detail.

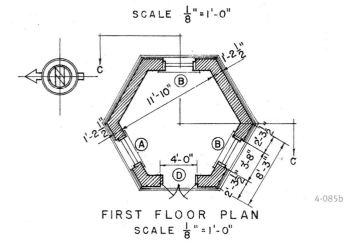

SCALE 1/8"=1'-0"

FIRST FLOOR PLAN
SCALE 1/8"=1'-0"

4-085b

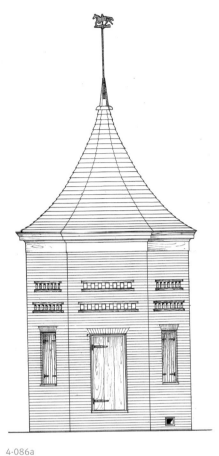

4-086a

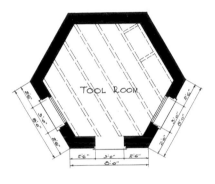

4-086b

4-086a. Front elevation of the dovecote, Angelina Plantation, Mt. Airy, St. John the Baptist Parish, Louisiana. H. H. Dowling, delineator, 1934. P & P, HABS, LA-18-14; HABS, LA,-MOTAI,V, 1- , sheet no. 1, detail.

4-086b. Floor plan of the dovecote, Angelina Plantation, Mt. Airy, St. John the Baptist Parish, Louisiana. H. H. Dowling, delineator, 1934. P & P, HABS, LA-18-14; HABS, LA,-MOTAI,V, 1- , sheet no. 1, detail.

4-087. Dovecote, The Folly, Accomac Vic., Accomack County, Virginia. Jack E. Boucher, photographer, 1960. P & P, HABS, VA-633; HABS, VA, 1-AC.V, 2B-1.

4-087

4-088

4-089

4-090

4-088. Chicken coop near Manning, South Carolina. October, 1939. Marion Post Wolcott, photographer. P & P, LC-USF 33-30420-M2.

During the antebellum period chickens were typically allowed to range about the farm. But when chickens and eggs became an important source of supplementary income, they were provided with a shelter consisting of either a small log pen or a framed shed (4-089, 4-090).

4-089. Chicken coop, Coffee County, Alabama. April, 1939. Marion Post Wolcott, photographer. P & P, LC-USF 34-51459-D.

4-090. Chicken house at the Irwindale Farms, Irwindale, Georgia. August, 1935. John Vachon, photographer. P & P, LC-USF 33-1136-M1.

THE UPLAND SOUTH

ALABAMA, GEORGIA, KENTUCKY, MARYLAND, MISSISSIPPI, NORTH CAROLINA,

SOUTH CAROLINA, TENNESSEE, VIRGINIA, WEST VIRGINIA

UPLAND SOUTH FARMSCAPES

The upland South begins at the fall line, the point where the coastal plain meets the abrupt rise of the hilly Piedmont region. This rolling pastureland eventually merges with the great mountain ranges of the Blue Ridge, the Smokies, and the Appalachians. Up in the mountains there are few sizable parcels of level ground useful for farming except for the bottomlands tucked into steep-sided canyons or the windswept clearings that dot the Cumberland plateau. This rough landscape of hills and hollows, ridges and valleys, extends well above the Ohio River before giving way to the flat prairies of the Midwest. The upland South is a region of small farms where self-sufficiency is the prime goal; most farms contain less than a hundred acres on average. There are, to be sure, places in the upland South where cash crops are raised: tobacco in the Carolina Piedmont and the Kentucky

Bluegrass, for example. But the pattern of the upland South is focused on what might be best termed "general agriculture," a mix of livestock and feed grains.

While the upper South was settled by people moving inward from the coastal lowlands, this region was also strongly influenced by settlers traveling down into the so-called southern backcountry from southeastern Pennsylvania, a group that included considerable numbers of Germans and Scotch-Irish. Features of mountain life that are often considered emblematically southern—hewn log construction, the dulcimer, the long rifle— have Germanic origins. The typical log house, which is rectangular in plan rather than square like the English cottage, has Irish antecedents. The upland South is then a region marked by important cultural fusions and transformations.

The following images convey the spectrum of upland places, ranging from a clearing on the Cumberland Plateau (5-001) to a farm standing in the shadow of the Blue Ridge mountains (5-002). Upland South farms, like those of the lowlands, were not rigorously planned. Barns and other structures were generally scattered about in an ad-hoc manner (5-003–5-006, 5-008). In the settlements with high numbers of Germans—such as those found in central Maryland and on into the Shenandoah Valley—farms show strong ties to Pennsylvania with their bank barns and tight linear arrangements (5-008 and 5-009).

5-001. Farm near Barbourville, Kentucky.
November, 1940. Marion Post Wolcott, photographer. P & P, LC-USF 34-56428-D.

5-002. Farm on the Hughes River at the base
of the Blue Ridge Mountains, Madison
County, Virginia. October, 1935. Arthur
Rothstein, photographer. P & P, LC-USF 34-
000359-D.

5-001

5-002

5-003

5-004

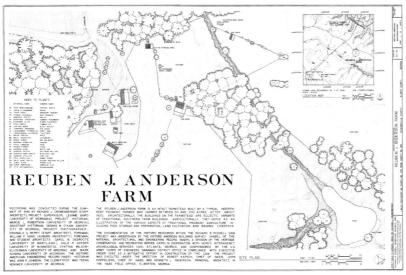

5-005

5-003. Jett's Farm, Falmouth, Stafford Co., Virginia. Frances Benjamin Johnston, photographer, ca. 1930. P & P, LC-J7-VA-2822.

5-004. Farm near Radford, Virginia. October, 1941. Marion Post Wolcott, photographer. P & P, LC-USF 34-090203-D.

5-005. Site plan, Reuben J. Anderson Farm, Ruckersville Vic., Elbert County, Georgia. Dale R. Gerber, Richard J. Cronberger, delineators, 1980. P & P, HABS, GA-32; HABS, GA, 53-RUCK.V, 2- , sheet no. 1.

The plan of the Anderson farm illustrates the usual plan of a southern farm: a simple residence backed by a semi-circle of agricultural buildings. These include in this instance a cow barn, mule barn, cotton shed, corncrib, and hayrack.

5-006. Corncrib and mule barn, Reuben J. Anderson Farm, Ruckersville Vic., Elbert County, Georgia. Dennis O'Kain, photographer, 1980. P & P, HABS, GA-32; HABS, GA, 53-RUCK.V, 2-10.

5-007. Cow barn, Reuben J. Anderson Farm, Ruckersville Vic., Elbert County, Georgia. Dennis O'Kain, photographer, 1980. P & P, HABS, GA-32; HABS, GA, 53-RUCK.V, 3-10.

5-008. Farm near Frederick, Maryland. February, 1940. Marion Post Wolcott, photographer. P & P, LC-USF 34-52914-D.

5-006

5-007

5-008

5-009

5-009. Shenandoah Valley farm, Virginia. May, 1941. Marion Post Wolcott, photographer. P & P, LC-USF 34-057503-D.

To assess the fertility of this valley farm, compare this image with the mountain scene in 5-001.

Single-unit barns could be arranged in at least three ways: gables set to the sides (5-010–5-012), gable to the front (5-013 and 5-014), and gable to the front with sheds attached to the sides (5-015–5-017). In the last configuration two modes of storage are provided; animals or grain inside, and tools and other equipment outside.

5-010

5-010. Dairy barn, Harper-Featherstone Farm, Lowndesville, Abbeville County, South Carolina. Dennis O'Kain, photographer, 1980. P & P, HABS, SC-379-B; HABS, SC, 1-LOWN.V, 1B-1.

5-011. Small barn near Stem, North Carolina. November, 1939. Marion Post Wolcott, photographer. P & P, LC-USF 34-30722-M4.

5-011

5-012

5-013

5-014

5-012. Stallion barns at Fairvue farm, Gallatin Vic., Sumner County, Tennessee. Jack E. Boucher, photographer, November, 1971. P & P, HABS TN-80-B; HABS, TENN, 83-GAL.V, IB-1.

5-013. Frame barn, Green Hill Plantation, Long Island Vic., Campbell County, Virginia. Jack E. Boucher, photographer, 1960. P & P, HABS, VA-610; HABS, VA, 15-LONI.V, 1M-1.

5-014. Log barn, Green Hill Plantation, Long Island Vic., Campbell County, Virginia. Jack E. Boucher, photographer, 1960. P & P, HABS, VA-611; HABS, VA, 15-LONI.V, 1N-1.

5-015. Log barn, Williams Place, Glen Springs, Spartanburg County, South Carolina. Jack E. Boucher, photographer, 1987. P & P, HABS, SC-615-F; HABS, SC, 42-GLENS, 1F-4.

5-016. Barn, Walker Farm, Gatlinburg, Sevier County, Tennessee. Edouard E. Exline, photographer, 1936. P & P, HABS, TN-121-C; HABS, TENN, 78-GAT, 1C-4.

5-017. Barn, Hill of Howth Plantation, Boligee Vic., Greene County, Alabama. Alex Bush, photographer, 1935. P & P, HABS, ALA-208; HABS, ALA, 32-BOLI.V, 1-9.

5-015

5-016

5-017

DOUBLE-CRIB BARNS AND THREE-BAY BARNS

Adding another crib to the single-crib barn resulted in a structure that was the spatial equivalent of a three-bay barn if a space was left between the two cribs (5-018, 5-022–5-026). If the cribs stood next to one another, the barn was functionally a large single-crib barn with a rectangular floorplan (5-021).

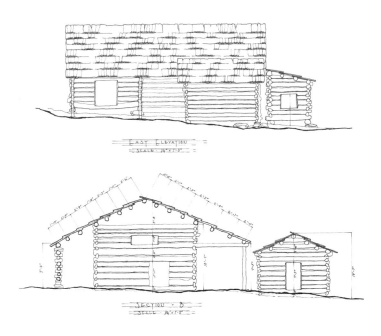

5-018

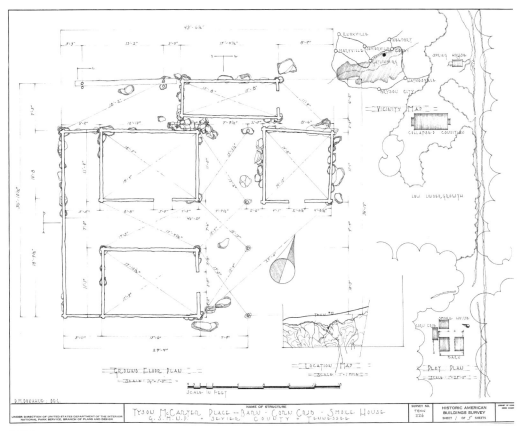

5-019

5-018. East elevation and sections, log barn, Tyson McCarter Place, Gatlinburg Vic., Sevier County, Tennessee. D. M. Donahue, delineator, ca. 1960. P & P, HABS, TN-226; HABS, TENN, 78-GAT.V, 5A-, sheet no. 3.

5-019. Floor plan, log barn, Tyson McCarter Place, Gatlinburg Vic., Sevier County, Tennessee. D. M. Donahue, delineator, ca. 1960. P & P, HABS, TN-266; HABS, TENN, 78-GAT.V, 5A-, sheet no. 1.

This sheet shows how log pens of different sizes are used to create a barn, a corncrib (the very narrow crib), and a smokehouse (the square crib just in front of the barn).

5-020. Log barn, Hikes Place, Jefferson County, Kentucky. Lester Jones, photographer, 1940. P & P, HABS, KY-70; HABS, KY, 56-BEUCH.V, 1-4.

5-021. Floor plan, west elevation, and south elevation, M. V. Riddle barn, Tishomingo Vic., Tishomingo County, Mississippi. Richard Cronenberger, Daniel Gaines, delineators, 1978. P & P, HABS, MS-180; HABS, MISS, 71-TISH.V, 9- , sheet no. 2.

The Riddle barn is organized more like a single-crib barn even though it is composed of two cribs. Without a central passage, it resembles a log barn composed of a rectangular crib flanked by sheds (compare with 5-015).

5-020

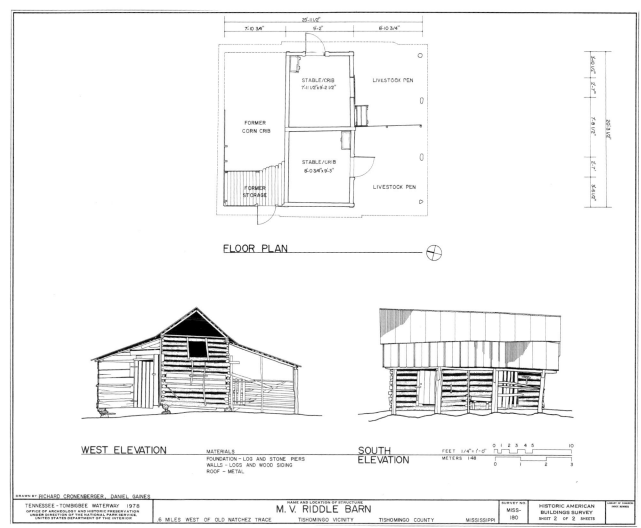

5-021

5-022

5-022. Log barn, Rockingham County, North Carolina. Frances Benjamin Johnston, 1938. P & P, LC-J7-NC-2954.

Some double-crib barns, like this one, were created incrementally by adding a crib to the gable end of the first crib.

5-023. Barn between Elkins and Morgantown, West Virginia, September, 1938. Marion Post Wolcott, photographer. P & P, LC-USF 34-050095-E.

5-024. Barn, Walker Family Farm, Gatlinburg, Sevier County, Tennessee. Edouard R. Exline, photographer, 1930s. P & P, HABS, TN-121-E; HABS, TENN, 78-GATR, 1E-1.

5-023

5-024

5-025

5-025. Log barn, Belmont Plantation, Spring Valley Vic., Colbert County, Alabama. Alex Bush, photographer, 1936. P & P, HABS, ALA-388; HABS, ALA, 17-SPRIVA.V, 1-43.

5-026. Log barn, Lowndesville Vic., Abbeville County, South Carolina. Dennis O'Kain, photographer, 1980. P & P, HABS, SC-383B-2; HABS, SC, 1-LOWN.V, 5B-2.

5-026

5-027

5-027. Barn, Burke County, North Carolina. Frances Benjamin Johnston, photographer, 1938. P & P, LC-J7-NC-2071.

5-028. Davidson barn, Charlotte Vic., Mecklenburg County, North Carolina. Frances Benjamin Johnston, photographer, 1938. P & P, LC-J7-NC-2643.

5-028

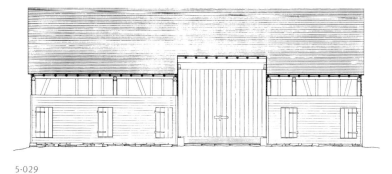

5-029

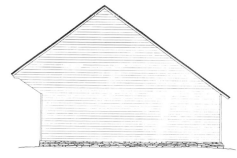

5-030

5-029. East elevation, Jones livestock barn, Bethania, Forsyth County, North Carolina. M. G. Marshall, W. W. Jones, delineators, 1962. P & P, HABS, NC-240; HABS, NC, 34-BETH, 1A- , sheet no. 4.

Bethania was settled principally by German-speaking Moravians who came to the back-country of North Carolina from Bethlehem, Pennsylvania, in 1759. This group joined a significant stream of Pennsylvania settlers who were moving into the south via the Shenandoah Valley of Virginia.

5-030. North elevation, Jones livestock barn, Bethania, Forsyth County, North Carolina. M. G. Marshall, W. W. Jones, delineators, 1962. P & P, HABS, NC-240; HABS, NC, 34-BETH, 1A- , sheet no. 1.

5-031. Plan of the loft level, Jones livestock barn, Bethania, Forsyth County, North Carolina. M. G. Marshall, W. W. Jones, delineators, 1962. P & P, HABS, NC-240; HABS, NC, 34-BETH, 1A- , sheet no. 3.

The plan clearly shows the three major components of the barn: a central passage flanked by storage and stabling areas.

5-032. Barn, Poplar Forest, Bedford Vic., Bedford County, Virginia. Jack E. Boucher, photographer, 1987. P & P, HABS, VA-303-D; HABS, VA, 10-BED.V, 1D-4.

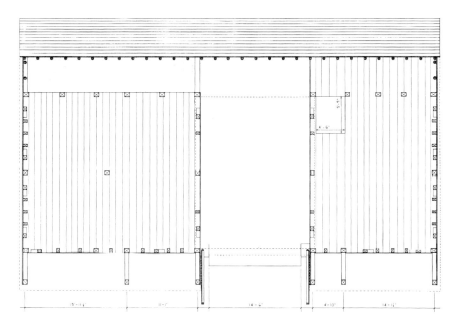

5-031

5-032

FOUR-CRIB AND CANTILEVERED LOG BARNS

A four-crib barn consists of two double-crib barns, one set behind the other. Often arranged with a space between the front and rear halves, the four-crib barns were crossed with two passages, one running from front to back, the other from gable to gable. At some point farmers realized that this cruciform pattern of passageways wasted crucial storage space and eventually, perhaps at the beginning of the nineteenth century, one of the passages was routinely closed off, producing the first transverse-crib barns (see 5-037).

5-033

5-034

5-033. Junglebrook barn, Gatlinburg Vic., Sevier County, Tennessee. Jack E. Boucher, photographer, 1958. P & P, HABS, TN-123; HABS, TENN, 78-GAT.V, 2B-1.

5-034. Witt Shields barn, Cades Cove, Blount County, Tennessee. Charles S. Grossman, photographer, 1937. P & P, HABS, TN-160; HABS, TENN, 5-CADCO, 3A-2.

Along the eastern border of Tennessee, particularly in Blount and Sevier Counties, barn builders were extraordinarily innovative in the way that they modified the common double-crib barn. They began by constructing cribs that were two stories high and then created extra storage space on the second level by extending the beams that supported the loft floor as much as ten feet beyond the walls of the cribs. When these cantilevered beams reached out beyond all four sides of the building, the upper level effectively formed a huge wooden canopy over the lower half of the barn.

Built first as early as 1815, more than 300 cantilevered log barns are still standing in eastern Tennessee. The Witt Shields barn is one of the more complicated of these barns. The floor plan (5-035) reveals that numerous cribs have been added, over the years, to the front and to the sides of the barn. Thus the cantilevered overhang can only be seen along the back of the barn. The transverse section (5-036b) and the plan (5-035) make clear that at the core of this huge barn building there stands only a modest double-crib structure.

5-035a. Longitudinal section, Witt Shields barn, Cades Cove, Tennessee. No delineator or date indicated. P & P, HABS, TN-160; HABS, TENN, 5-CADCO, 3A-, sheet no. 4, detail.

5-035b. Transverse section, Witt Shields barn, Cades Cove, Tennessee. No delineator or date indicated. P & P, HABS, TN-160; HABS, TENN, 5-CADCO, 3A-, sheet no. 4, detail.

5-036. Floor plan, Witt Shields barn, Cades Cove, Tennessee. No delineator or date indicated. P & P, HABS, TN-160; HABS, TENN, 5-CADCO, 3A-, sheet no. 1.

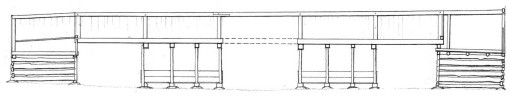

5-035a

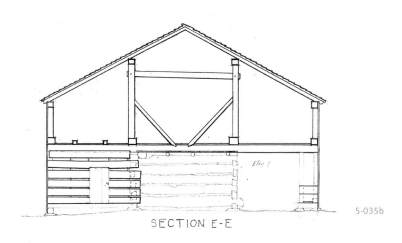

SECTION E-E

5-035b

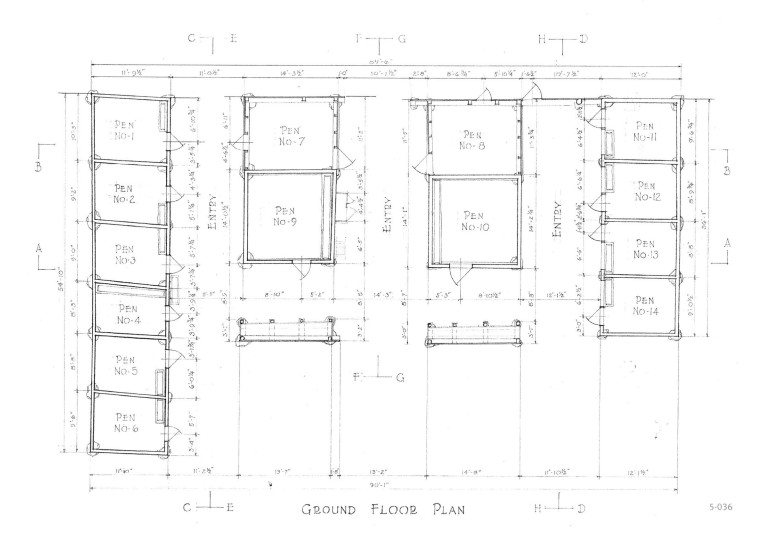

GROUND FLOOR PLAN

5-036

TRANSVERSE-CRIB BARNS

The transverse-crib barn is thought to have been invented in the Wautaga area at the headwaters of a tributary to the great Tennessee River early in the nineteenth century. The Tennessee River Valley was one of the few zones of the upland South blessed with rich limestone-derived soils and thus it contained the most productive farms. Backcountry farmers who recognized that it was possible to raise large herds quickly saw the need for large barns. Since none of the traditional forms in the crib-based tradition was adequate, they began to experiment to find a satisfactory alternative. Converting the eaves side–opening four-crib (5-033) barn into a multicrib barn with its entrances in its gable ends (5-037–5-041) was a simple but important modification. It required only the closing of the passages on the eaves sides, but the effect of this design move was quite radical, for it produced a new barn that was well adapted for efficient cattle raising. The barn offered easy access to all of the stabling areas and, with the hay stored above the stalls, the cows' feed could be dropped easily into their mangers. Should the barn ever need to be expanded, more cribs could be added without upsetting the existing circulation patterns within the barn. Sheds could be added along the outer walls (5-042–5-052), or the depth of the barn could be increased by building additional pairs of cribs at the rear of the building. In theory a transverse-crib barn could have an unlimited number of cribs; in actual practice they rarely contained more than ten.

5-037

5-037. Log barn, Walker County, Alabama. February, 1937. Arthur Rothstein, photographer. P & P, LC-USF 34-025125-D.

5-038. Barn, Adam Clement Farm, Doughton Park Vic., Wilkes County, North Carolina. Pat Mullen, photographer, 1978. AFC, Blue Ridge Parkway Folklife Survey, Blue Ridge 4-20189, no. 22.

5-039. Barn, Truitt Farm, Allegheny County, North Carolina. Blanton Owen, photographer, 1978. AFC, Blue Ridge Parkway Folklife Survey, Blue Ridge 5-20365, no. 5.

5-040. Stock barn, B. C. Corbett Farm, Carr, Orange County, North Carolina. November, 1939. Marion Post Wolcott, photographer. P & P, LC-USF 34-052050-D.

5-038

5-039

5-040

5-041

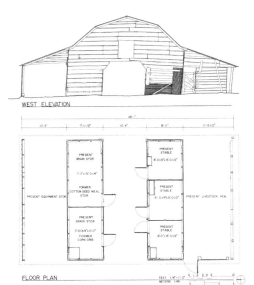

WEST ELEVATION

FLOOR PLAN

5-042

5-043

5-041. Barn, Morehead, Kentucky. July, 1940. Marion Post Wolcott, photographer. P & P, LC-USF 34-055430-D.

5-042. West elevation and floor plan, John R. Trimm barn, Tishomingo Vic., Tishomingo County, Mississippi. Ruthie Wiley, delineator, 1978. P & P, HABS, MS-181; HABS, MISS, 71-TISH.V, 10- , sheet no. 2.

5-043. Cube Walker barn, Belzoni, Mississippi. November, 1939. Marion Post Wolcott, photographer. P & P, LC-USF 34-052270-D.

5-044. Barn, Woolwine Vic., Patrick County, Virginia. Howard Wight Marshall, photographer, 1978. AFC, Blue Ridge Parkway Folklife Survey, Blue Ridge 2-20205, no. 9.

5-044

5-045. Patton barn, Florence Vic., Lauderdale County, Alabama. Alex Bush, photographer, 1935. P & P, HABS, ALA-333; HABS, ALA, 39-FLO.V, 2-10.

5-046. Stencil House barn, Clifton Vic., Wayne County, Tennessee. Jack E. Boucher, photographer, 1974. P & P, HABS, TN-190-A; HABS, TENN, 91-CLIF.V, 1A-2.

5-047. Barn, Pond Spring Plantation, Wheeler Station, Lawrence County, Alabama. Alex Bush, photographer, 1935. P & P, HABS, ALA-347; HABS, ALA, 40-WHEL, 1-12.

5-045

5-046

5-047

5-048

5-049

5-050

5-048. Barn, Laurel Fork Vic., Carroll County, Virginia. Howard Wight Marshall, photographer, 1978. AFC, Blue Ridge Parkway Folklife Survey, Blue Ridge 2-20198, no. 6.

5-049. Williams Place frame barn, Glen Springs, Spartanburg County, South Carolina. Jack E. Boucher, photographer, 1987. P & P, HABS, SC-614-C; HABS, SC, 42-GLENS, 1C-2.

With careful planning the extra sheds on the sides of a transverse-crib barn could be integrated into the design of the building without necessitating a change in the roof line. Barns like this one with three openings across the front facade are sometimes referred to as "three-portal barns."

5-050. Barn, Poplar Forest, Bedford Vic, Bedford County, Virginia. Jack E. Boucher, photographer, 1987. P & P, HABS, VA-303-D; HABS, VA, 10-BED.V, 1D-2.

The lines of this barn recall the profile of the Louisiana "trinity" barn (4-016), but this barn is considerably larger and built to shelter several teams rather than one or two horses.

5-051. Barn, Chesterfield County, Virginia. Frances Benjamin Johnston, photographer, 1931. P & P, LC-J7-VA-1631.

5-052. Barn, Waynesville, Swain County, North Carolina. Jack E. Boucher, photographer, 1960. P & P, HABS, NC-390-B; HABS, NC, 87-WAVI.V, 1-B-1.

The large frame roof used here to provide a commodious haymow over a set of log cribs suggests an awareness of the cantilevered barns of eastern Tennessee. Because Swain County, North Carolina, shares a border with Sevier County, Tennessee, it is quite possible that the builder of this barn had seen cantilevered barns with their distinctive extended eaves.

5-053. Barn, Absher Vic., Wilkes County, North Carolina. Blanton Owen, photographer, 1978. AFC, Blue Ridge Parkway Folklife Survey, Blue Ridge 3-20365, no. 3.

Taking full advantage of a hillside location, the builder of this barn created direct outside access to the upper level. In so doing, he effectively turned a commonplace transverse-crib barn into an unusual bank barn.

5-051

5-052

5-053

5-054

5-054. Dairy barn, Radford, Virginia. October, 1941, Marion Post Wolcott, photographer. P & P, LC-USF 34-090237-D.

Dairy barns like this one, built during the first quarter of the twentieth century, were relatively narrow in order allow more light into the center of the barn. This modification is credited to designers at the University of Wisconsin's Agricultural Experiment Station some time around 1915. However, in plan such buildings clearly belong to the family of transverse-crib barns; they have gable entrances, central passages flanked by pairs of milking stalls, and a sizable hayloft overhead.

5-055. Dairy barn, Moatview Farm, poss. Lynchburg, Virginia. Bell Studio, 1924. P & P, Specific Subject File—Farm Buildings.

In the largest dairy barns the building often stretched to a length of more than 100 feet (and in some cases they were even longer). But even when transformed in this way, the beneficial qualities of the central passageway were never forsaken. The invention of milking machines, mechanical hay forks that ran on tracks suspended from the apex of the roof, and manure carts that ran behind the stalls meant there was no longer a conventional length for a dairy barn.

5-056. Barn, Bracketts Farm, Trevilians Vic., Louisa County, Virginia. Jack E. Boucher, photographer, 1983. P & P, HABS, VA-1215-E; HABS, VA, 55-TREV.V, 1E-1.

5-055

5-056

Air-cured varieties of tobacco are grown in some portions of the Piedmont areas of southern Virginia (5-057) but the majority of the air-cured tobacco grown in the upland South is raised in the Bluegrass region (5-058) and adjacent mountain sections of Kentucky.

5-057

5-057. Tobacco barn, Green Hill Plantation, Long Island Vic., Campbell County, Virginia, Jack E. Boucher, photographer, 1960. P & P, HABS, VA-614; HABS, VA, 16-LONI,V, 1D-1.

The size of this barn implies that considerable acreage at Green Hill Plantation was devoted to raising tobacco. At the height of Green Hill's operations, owner Samuel Panhill controlled more than 5,000 acres with at least 1,000 in cultivation in any one year.

5-058. Russell Spear's burley tobacco barn. Lexington, Kentucky. 1940. Marion Post Wolcott, photographer. P & P, LC-USF 34-055398-D.

Several types of tobacco barns appear in Kentucky. They vary in height, width, and type of ventilators. Many of them are painted black, like this one from the Bluegrass region. This color absorbs more of the sun's heat and thus the time required to dry the tobacco leaves is considerably shortened.

5-058

FLUE CURED–TOBACCO BARNS

Flue-cured tobacco is grown throughout the Piedmont section of the Carolinas. The barns used to dry the tobacco leaves are identical to the flue cured–tobacco barns encountered in the lowland sections of these states. The shift in topography and climate from one region to the other is not profound enough to require any significant changes in the way that the plant is grown or processed.

5-059

5-059. Tobacco barn near Gordonton, Person County, North Carolina, 1939. Dorothea Lange, photographer. P & P, LC-USF 34-019986-C.

Compare this barn and the next two examples (5-060 and 5-061) with the flue-cured tobacco barns from the lowland South (4-033–4-038).

5-060

5-060. Tobacco barn, Person County, North Carolina, 1939. Dorothea Lange, photographer. P & P, LC-USF 34-020028-C.

5-061. Tobacco barn, Prospect Hill, Caswell County, North Carolina, 1940. Marion Post Wolcott, photographer. P & P, LC-USF 34-056221-D.

5-062. Tobacco stripping house near Stem, North Carolina. November, 1939. Marion Post Wolcott, photographer. P & P, LC-USF 34-52608-D.

Usually workers sat under sheds next to the barn while they stripped the tobacco leaves from their stalks before the leaves were hung up in the barn to be dried. At this farm, they were provided with a separate building.

5-061

5-062

Settlers from Pennsylvania brought the bank barn into the upland South as they moved southward across Maryland toward the Shenandoah Valley of Virginia. The path of their migration can be traced by the trail of large bank barns that stand out so clearly on their farms (see 5-009).

5-063

5-063. Hilliard's Farm barn, Jefferson County, West Virginia. Ian McLaughlin, photographer, 1936. P & P, HABS, WVA-32; HABS, WVA,19-DARK.V, 2A-2.

Even though West Virginians like to refer to themselves as mountaineers, Jefferson County lies within the Shenandoah Valley. Because the physical landscape of this area resembles southeastern Pennsylvania in many ways, it was easy for settlers from the Mid-Atlantic to deploy familiar agricultural practices. The barns like the one at Hilliard's Farm can easily be traced back to the heart of the Pennsylvania Dutch country (compare with 3-061).

5-064

5-065

5-066

5-064. Ramp view of the Lee barn, Jefferson County, West Virginia. Ian McLaughlin, photographer, 1936. P & P, HABS, WVA-4; HABS, WVA, 19-LETO, 1AB-2.

This end wall–supported forebay barn (also known as a closed forebay barn) is identical to examples from Pennsylvania (compare 3-077–3-085).

5-065. Forebay view of the Lee barn, Jefferson County, West Virginia. Ian McLaughlin, photographer, 1936. P & P, HABS, WVA-4; HABS, WVA, 19-LETO, 1AB-3.

5-066. Philip Pry Farm barn, Washington County, Maryland. Jack E. Boucher, photographer, 1989. P & P, HABS, MD-864-A; HABS, MD, 22-SHARP.V, 8-A-1.

That Maryland would share barn types with Pennsylvania is not surprising, since they are neighboring states. Further, in their migration down into the Shenandoah Valley, thousands of Germans traveled across Maryland. Clearly many of them, to judge from the barns found in Maryland, decided that they had traveled far enough (see 5-067–5-075).

5-067. Auburn barn, Sandy Springs, Montgomery County, Maryland. John O. Brostrup, photographer, 1936. P & P, HABS, MD-597; HABS, MD, 16-SANSP, 2A-1.

5-068. Gorsuch barn, Hereford Vic., Baltimore County, Maryland. E. H. Pickering, photographer, 1936. P & P, HABS, MD-1; HABS, MD, 3-____, 2-4.

5-069. Decorative ventilators on the Gorsuch Barn, Baltimore County, Maryland. Frances Benjamin Johnston, photographer, 1936–37. P & P, LA-J7-MD-1033.

5-067

5-068

5-069

5-070

5-070. Bank barn near Hagerstown, Maryland. October, 1936. Arthur Rothstein, photographer. P & P, LC-USF 34-005556-E.

5-071. Bank barn near Frederick, Maryland. February, 1940. Marion Post Wolcott, photographer. P & P, LC-USF 34-52918-D.

5-071

5-072. Bank barn, Blendon Estate, Owings Mills Vic., Baltimore County, Maryland. Martin Stupich, photographer, 1989. P & P, HABS, MD-994-B; HABS, MD, 3-OWMI.V, 3-B-8.

5-073. Samuel Gaither barn, Unity Vic., Montgomery County, Maryland. John O. Brostrup, photographer, 1936. P & P, HABS, MD-108; HABS, MD, 16-UNI.V, 1A-2.

5-074. Henry Rohrbach barn, Sharpsburg Vic., Washington County, Maryland. Jack E. Boucher, photographer, 1984. P & P, HABS MD-994-A; HABS, MD, 22-SHARP.V, 24-A-2.

5-072

5-073

5-074

5-075

5-075. Barn, Woodlawn Manor, Norwood, Montgomery County, Maryland. John O. Brostrup, photographer, 1936. P & P, HABS, MD-578; HABS, MD, 16-NORWO, 1-3.

The great double-decker, stone-arched forebay barn at Norwood rivals the most impressive barns from Pennsylvania (compare with 3-082–3-083.)

5-076. Harnsbarger barn, Grottoes Vic., Augusta County, Virginia. Jack E. Boucher, photographer, 1971. P & P, HABS, VA-1211; HABS, VA, 8-GROTT.V, 1-2.

This octagonal barn was built during the period when such structures were considered progressive innovations. Yet, in this barn the force of traditional ideas remains strong. Sharing the territory with German forebay barns, the builder opted to site the barn on sloping ground and recess the downhill foundation to create a post-supported forebay. He ended up with an octagonal bank barn.

5-076

OTHER BARNS

5-077. Barn and farm buildings, Hayfields, Cockeysville Vic., Baltimore County, Maryland. E. H. Pickering, photographer, 1936. P & P, HABS, MD-15; HABS, MD, 3-COCK.V, 1-15.

The barn at Hayfields represents a mixing of German and English influences. The barn is a two-level barn with feed storage placed over a stable, but it has no ramp to the upper level. Thus, it looks like a bank barn but operates like an English three-bay barn. In place of a forebay it had a pent roof that wrapped around three sides of the barn. This protective awning resembled the roofs appended to English bank barns from the Lake District but here there was only one centrally located door rather than a series of stable entrances. The Hayfields barn is intriguingly unique and yet familiar.

5-078. Plan, Hayfields farm buildings, Cockeysville Vic., Baltimore County, Maryland. Robert E. Lewis, delineator, 1936. P & P, HABS, MD-15; HABS, MD, 3-COCK.V, 1- , sheet no. 2.

5-077

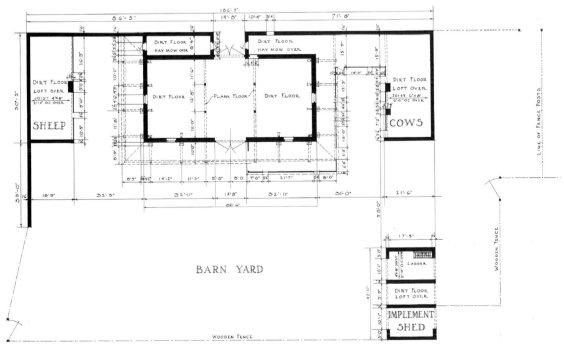

SCALE 1/16-1'-0"

BARN YARD

5-078

5-079

5-079. View under the pent roof on the front of the Hayfields barn, Cockeysville Vic., Baltimore County, Maryland. E. H. Pickering, photographer, 1936. P & P, HABS, MD-15; HABS, MD, 3-COCK.V, 1-18.

5-080. Cow barn, Hampton, Towson Vic., Baltimore County, Maryland. E. H. Pickering, photographer, 1936. P & P, HABS, MD-226-H; HABS, MD, 3-TOW.V, 1U-1.

This large stone barn is an addition to what once was little more than a line of horse stalls. The plan for this barn (5-081) reveals that after half of the stable was demolished, a larger cow barn was appended to the remaining portion. The two buildings were arranged in an L-shaped configuration. After a series of sheds was added inside the bend of the angle, the net result was a unique barn crafted from standard components.

5-080

5-093. Stable, River View, Seneca Vic., Montgomery County, Maryland. John O. Brostrup, photographer, 1936. P & P, HABS, MD-604; HABS, MD, 16-SENCA.V, 2-5.

5-094. Plan, James Ben Ali Haggin horse barn, Lexington, Fayette County, Kentucky. Tim Winters, delineator, 1984. P & P, HABS, KY-171; HABS, KY, 34-LEX, 11A- , sheet no. 3.

5-095. Section of a typical stall in the James Ben Ali Haggin horse barn, Lexington, Fayette County, Kentucky. Tim Winters, delineator, 1984. P & P, HABS, KY-171; HABS, KY, 34-LEX, 11A- , sheet no. 7.

5-093

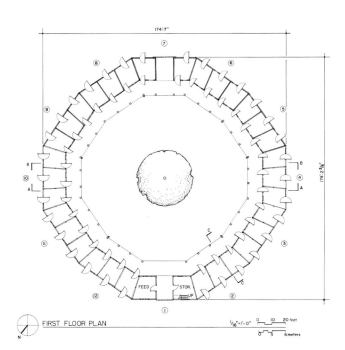

5-094

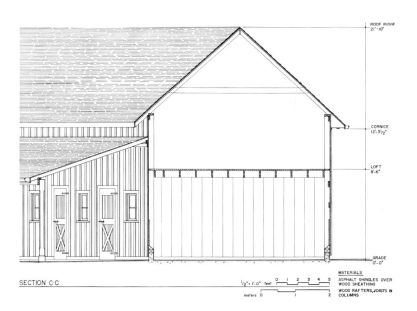

5-095

HAYSTACKS

In the South, hay and fodder can be successfully stored in stacks piled up out in the open but it was still necessary to construct the stack carefully and to protect it from animals and the wind. Haystacks were constructed around a central pole (called a stackpole) and occasionally barricaded inside a rail fence.

5-096

5-097

5-096. Haystacks and shocks of corn, Marion, Virginia. May, 1941. Marion Post Wolcott, photographer. P & P, LC-USF 34-056093-D.

The corn shocks are silhouetted on the distant hill in the background.

5-097. Haystacks, Mineral County, West Virginia. February, 1940. Arthur Rothstein, photographer. P & P, LC-USF 34-029359-D.

5-098. Haystacks and wall of fodder near a barn, Caswell County, North Carolina. September, 1936. Marion Post Wolcott, photographer. P & P, LC-USF 34-052048-D.

The huge pile of corn husks next to the barn was placed there as a supply of bedding for animals.

5-098

In the upland South, as in its lowland counterpart, corn is a staple. Hence the corncrib was a standard outbuilding in the region. In keeping with the strong regional tradition of hewn log construction, the corncrib was often a tightly fitted pen of logs (5-099–5-103). When more storage space was needed, two log cribs were arranged into a drive-through building which also served as an equipment shelter (5-104 and 5-105).

5-099

5-100

5-099. Corncrib, Waynesville Vic., Swain County, North Carolina. Jack E. Boucher, photographer, 1960. P & P, HABS, NC-390-C; HABS, NC, 87-WAVI.V, 1-C-1.

5-100. Corncrib, Bracketts Farm, Trevilians Vic., Louisa County, Virginia. Jack E. Boucher, photographer, 1983. P & P, HABS, VA-1215-F; HABS, VA, 55-TREV.V, 1F-1.

5-101

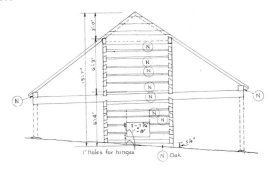

WEST ELEVATION
Scale-¼"=1'-0"

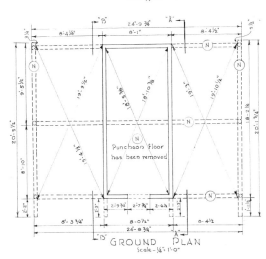

GROUND PLAN
Scale-¼"=1'-0"

5-102

5-103

5-101. Corncrib, Falling Green, Olney Vic., Montgomery County, Maryland. John O. Brostrup, photographer, 1936. P & P, HABS, MD-580; HABS, MD, 16-OLNEY.V, 1-18.

5-102. West elevation and plan, Garland Townsend corncrib, Cades Cove, Blount County, Tennessee. Delineator unknown, 1937. P & P, HABS, TN-119; HABS, TENN, 5-CADCO, 2A-, sheet no. 1.

5 103. Stencil House corncrib, Clifton Vic., Wayne County, Tennessee. Jack E. Boucher, photographer, 1979. P & P, HABS, TN-190-B; HABS, TENN, 91-CLIF.V, 1B-1.

5-104. Hall House corncrib, Carroll County, Virginia. Blanton Owen, photographer, 1978. AFC, Blue Ridge Parkway Folklife Survey, Blue Ridge 7-20169, no. 16.

5-105. Mc Clure Cabin corncrib, Rutherford County, North Carolina. Frances Benjamin Johnston, photographer, 1938. P & P, LC-J7-NC-2944.

5-106. Corncrib, Hampton, Towson Vic., Baltimore County, Maryland. Lenny Miyamoto, photographer, 1959. P & P, HABS, MD-226-N; HABS, MD, 3-TOW.V, 1W-1.

5-104

5-105

5-106

5-107

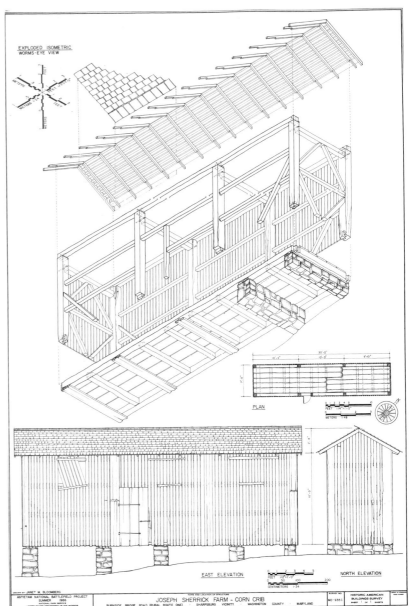

EXPLODED ISOMETRIC
WORMS-EYE VIEW

PLAN

EAST ELEVATION

NORTH ELEVATION

DRAWN BY: JANET M. BLOOMBERG
ANTIETAM NATIONAL BATTLEFIELD PROJECT
SUMMER 1986
NATIONAL PARK SERVICE
UNITED STATES DEPARTMENT OF THE INTERIOR

JOSEPH SHERRICK FARM - CORN CRIB
BURNSIDE BRIDGE ROAD (RURAL ROUTE ONE) - SHARPSBURG VICINITY - WASHINGTON COUNTY - MARYLAND

HISTORIC AMERICAN
BUILDINGS SURVEY
SHEET 1 OF 1 SHEETS

5-108

5-109

5-107. Corncrib near Bartlett, West Virginia. May, 1936. Taylor, photographer. P & P, LC-USF 34-014095.

In those states that border on the Mid-Atlantic region, narrow Pennsylvania-style cribs are encountered (compare this image and 5-108 with 3-103–3-104).

5-108. Isometric drawing, east elevation, and north elevation of the Sherrick House corncrib, Sharpsburg Vic., Washington County, Maryland. Janet M. Bloomberg, delineator, 1986. P & P, HABS, MD- 935-C; HABS, MD, 22-SHARP.V, 3C- , sheet no. 1.

5-109. Kenmuir corncrib, Trevilians Vic., Louisa County, Virginia. Jack E. Boucher, photographer, 1984. P & P, HABS, VA-1229-E; HABS, VA, 55-TRE.V, 8E-1.

5-110. Green River Plantation corncrib, Polk County, North Carolina. Frances Benjamin Johnston, photographer, 1938. P & P, LC-J7-NC-2837.

5-111. Hard Bargain corncrib, Northumberland County, Virginia. Frances Benjamin Johnston, photographer, 1935. P & P, LC-J7-VA-2266.

5-112a. North elevation, corncrib, Washington Hall, Washington, Mason County, Kentucky. Perry Benson, delineator, 1975. P & P, HABS, KY-131-A; HABS, KY, 81-WASH, 10A-, sheet no. 1.

This metal corncrib, fabricated by Martin Steel Products Company of Mansfield, Ohio, in 1919, suggests the arrival of a new age of agribusiness that challenged traditional practices and the viability of the old-fashioned structures that went with them.

5-112b. East elevation, corncrib, Washington Hall, Washington, Mason County, Kentucky. Perry Benson, delineator, 1975. P & P, HABS, KY-131-A; HABS, KY, 81-WASH, 10A-, sheet no. 1, detail.

5-112c. Plan, corncrib, Washington Hall, Washington, Mason County, Kentucky. Perry Benson, delineator, 1975. P & P, HABS, KY-131-A; HABS, KY, 81-WASH, 10A-, sheet no. 1, detail.

5-110

5-111

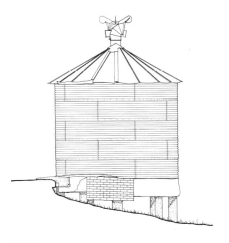

5-112a

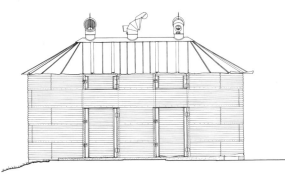

5-112b

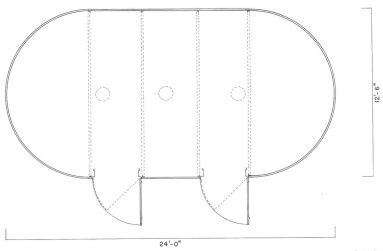

5-112c

5-113

5-113. Long barn–granary, Hampton, Towson Vic., Baltimore County, Maryland. Lenny Miyamoto, photographer, 1959. P & P, HABS, MD-226-G; HABS, MD, 3-TOW.V, 1T-1.

5-114. Dudley Snow House wheat house, Oxford, Calhoun County, Alabama. W. N. Manning, photographer, 1935. P & P, HABS, ALA-465; HABS, ALA, 8-OXFO, 1-9.

5-115. Pleasant Valley granary, Burke County, North Carolina. Frances Benjamin Johnston, photographer, 1938. P & P, LC-J7-NC-2074.

5-114

5-115

5-116. Granary, Green Hill Plantation, Long Island Vic., Campbell County, Virginia. Jack E. Boucher, photographer, 1960. P & P, HABS, VA-613; HABS, VA, 16-LONI,V, 1F-1.

5-117. Pigpen, Walker Family Farm, Gatlinburg, Sevier County, Tennessee. Edouard E. Exline, photographer, 1930s. P & P, HABS, TN-121-G; HABS, TENN, 78-GAT, 1G-1.

Pork was the meat of choice in nearly every southern household during the antebellum period and smoked hams remain a regional favorite celebratory item for holiday suppers. No self-sufficient farm could exist without a hog or two. This small log shelter represents a old-fashioned way to house a pig. Figure 5-118 presents an updated wood frame alternative covered with board-and-batten siding that was presumed to be better for the health of the pigs.

5-118. Hog pens on a farm near Elkins, West Virginia. August, 1936. Carl Mydans, photographer. P & P, LC-USF 33-726-M2.

5-116

5-117

5-118

THE MIDWEST

ILLINOIS, INDIANA, IOWA, MICHIGAN, MINNESOTA,

MISSOURI, OHIO, WISCONSIN

MIDWESTERN FARMSCAPES

The Midwest is certainly the most prolific agricultural region in the United States. Shaped by the force of successive glaciations, the terrain lay open and ready for the plow. Blessed with a thick layer of dark topsoil rich in humus, it is no wonder that the Midwest leads the nation in the production of feed grains and livestock. Often referred to as the Corn Belt, the region consists of more than fields of corn. Small farms devoted to general agriculture characterize the hilly southern tier of the region. Vast cornfields do extend across the region's middle section from Ohio to eastern Nebraska, while the dairy industry dominates in the Great Lakes states. These different types of farming are the result of differing histories of settlement. The southern sections of the Midwest were occupied by people moving in from the upland South, while the central Midwest was populated by settlers from the Mid-Atlantic region, mainly from Pennsylvania. The first generation of dairy farmers in Wisconsin and Michigan came principally from upstate New York and New England. Some scholars have argued that this mixing of populations marks the beginning of a single national identity by distilling the experience of consensus from an array of regional variations.

Midwestern farms are characterized, for the most part, by their orderliness, a regimen linked to the fixed grid of land division in the region. It was here that the 1785 federal survey system was first used. The land ordinance mandated that the so-called Northwest Territory (and subsequently the rest of the nation) be divided into square township blocks six miles on a side. These parcels were then subdivided into thirty-six sections, each of them a mile square containing 640 acres. Since this was considerably more land than most farmers were prepared to cultivate, the township sections were further divided into halves (320 acres), quarters (160 acres), and even quarter-quarters (40 acres). The resulting landscape consisted then of a territory marked by right angles and straight property lines running north to south and east to west. Within this national grid, farm plans were equally rigorous with tight clusters of buildings. Tied to the road system, farms were spaced at regular intervals and always faced one of the four cardinal directions. The overall feeling is one of consistency tied to a strong sense of order and conformity.

6-001. Farm near Dayton, Ohio. October,
1941. Marion Post Wolcott, photographer.
P & P, LC-USF 34-90053-D.

6-002. Stuart Brown's farm near Aledo,
Illinois. January, 1937. Russell Lee, photographer. P & P, LC-USF 341-10139-B.

6-001

6-002

LOG BARNS

In the northernmost part of the Midwest, which stretches across the top of Michigan, Wisconsin, and Minnesota, the lumber industry dominated. Here clear-cutting practices spawned the massive destruction of the woodlands and transformed the forests into a wasteland. In this area, which came to be known as the "Cut-over Region," a few hardy settlers attempted to develop farms using old pioneer practices that included the construction of log houses and barns (6-009–6-013).

6-009

6-010

6-011

6-009. Single log crib with sheds in the Cut-over region of northern Michigan. April, 1937. Russell Lee, photographer. P & P, LC-USF 341-T-010827-B.

6-010. Log barn near Winton, Minnesota. August, 1937. Russell Lee, photographer. P & P, LC-USF 34-030334-D.

6-011. Log barn near Tipler, Wisconsin. May, 1937. Russell Lee, photographer. P & P, LC-USF 341-010872-B.

6-012. Log barn in Iron County, Minnesota. May, 1937. Russell Lee, photographer. P & P, LC-USF 341-T-010840-B.

6-013. "Stove Wood" barn, Lena, Oconto County, Wisconsin. Photographer unknown, 1957. P & P, HABS, WI-286; HABS, WIS, 42-LENA, 1-2.

The stove-wood construction technique employs short pieces of wood as if they were bricks. Short pieces small enough to fit in a wood-burning stove are laid up in courses. The resulting walls have the look of a stacked pile of wood (see 1-056). In some cases, the corners will be constructed with larger hewn blocks and arranged in the manner of stone quoins. This building method is found most often in northeastern Wisconsin and may have its origins in the St. Lawrence Valley.

6-012

6-013

NEW ENGLAND-INFLUENCED BARNS

Settlers from New York with New England ancestors moved into the northern tier of the Midwest bringing with them designs for English three-bay barns (6-014 and 6-016) and the two-level gable-opening bank barn (6-018 and 6-019).

6-014

6-015

6-014. Clark Barn, Mequon, Ozaukee County, Wisconsin. John N. Vogel, photographer, 1988. P & P, HABS, WI-311-A; HABS, WIS, 45-MEQ, 1-A-3.

Note that this barn is finished with the same type of cobblestone veneer seen in upstate New York, an area identified by some geographers as New England Extended (compare 3-097).

6-015. General view of the Clark Farm, Mequon, Ozaukee County, Wisconsin. John N. Vogel, photographer, 1988. P & P, HABS, WI-311-A; HABS, WIS, 45-MEQ, 1-A-1.

Both barn and house are typical New England forms ornamented with Classical Revival style decorative touches which were dominant in the region well into the second quarter of the nineteenth century.

6-016. Barn near Marseilles, Illinois. Russell Lee, photographer, 1937. P & P, LC-USF 34-010163-D.

6-016

6-017. Olson Farm barn (front view), Bishop Hill, Henry County, Illinois. Ray Pearson, photographer, 1982. P & P, HABS, IL-169-Q; HABS, ILL, 37-BISH, 16-2.

Compare this with 1-001, 1-003, and 1-031.

6-018. Olson Farm barn (back view), Bishop Hill, Henry County, Illinois. Ray Pearson, photographer, 1982. P & P, HABS, IL-169-Q; HABS, ILL, 37-BISH, 16-3.

6-017

6-018

MID-ATLANTIC—INFLUENCED BANK BARNS

The influence of Mid-Atlantic custom was strongest in the central tier of the Midwest. Here readily identifiable barn types from Pennsylvania reappear (6-019–6-023). The imprint of upstate New York was felt most strongly in the northern dairy region; the two-level New York dairy barn is seen commonly in Michigan and Wisconsin (6-024–6-027).

6-019

6-020

6-019. Bank barn near Dayton, Ohio. July, 1938.
Dorothea Lange, photographer. P & P, LC-USF 34-9755-C.

6-020. Bank barn near Dayton, Ohio. October, 1941.
Marion Post Wolcott, photographer. P & P, LC-USF 34-090036-D.

6-021. Bank barn near Dayton, Ohio. October, 1941.
Marion Post Wolcott, photographer. P & P, LC-USF 34-090038-D.

6-021

6-022. Bank barn in central Ohio. Summer,
1938. Ben Shahn, photographer. P & P,
LC-USF 33-006643-M3.

6-023. Bank barn, Merit-Tandy Farm,
Patriot Vic., Switzerland County, Indiana.
Photographer unknown, 1982. P & P, HABS,
IN-195-B; HABS, IND, 78-PAT.V, 1B-1.

6-024

6-025

6-024. Bank barn near Inkster, Michigan. September, 1942. Arthur Siegel, photographer. P & P, LC-USW 3-9167-C.

6-025. Bank barn in Isabella County, Michigan. August, 1941. John Vachon, photographer. P & P, LC-USF 34-063735-D.

6-026. Bank barn in Door County, Wisconsin. July, 1940.
John Vachon, photographer. P & P, LC-USF 34-61260-D.

6-027. Bank barn near Madison, Wisconsin. July, 1937.
Russell Lee, photographer. P & P, LC-USF 34-30253-D.

6-028. Bank barn, Oliver Hudson Kelly Farm, Elk River Vic.,
Sherburne County, Minnesota. Jet Lowe, photographer, 1987.
P & P, HABS, MN-84A; HABS, MINN, 71-ELKR.V, 1-A-2.

6-026

6-027

6-028

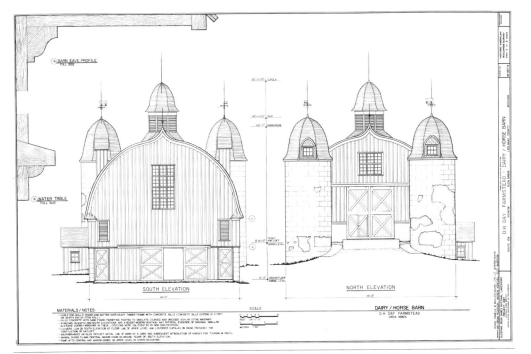

6-029

6-029. South and north elevations, dairy-horse barn, D. H. Day Farm, Glen Arbor, Leelanau County, Michigan. Pamela M. Mullen, Chelle Jenkins, Brian Pederson, Andrew Wenchel, Scott McBroom, delineators, 1987. P & P, HABS, MI-257-B; HABS, MICH, 45-GLAR, 12 B-, sheet no. 3.

This barn, which had a ramped entrance to the second level at its north end, combines the two-level arrangement of a nineteenth-century bank barn with the length and width of newer dairy barns which emerged around 1920 (compare with 6-057).

6-030. West elevation, dairy-horse barn, D. H. Day Farm, Glen Arbor, Leelanau County, Michigan. Ron Havelka, delineator, 1987. P & P, HABS, MI-257-B; HABS, MICH, 45-GLAR, 12 B-, sheet no. 4.

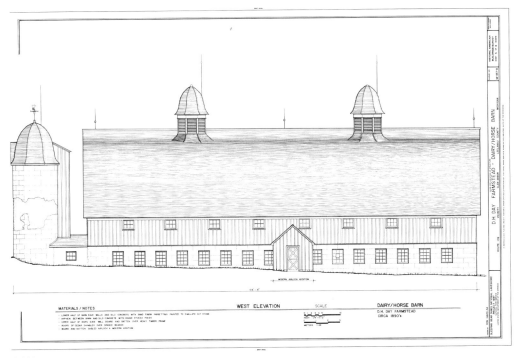

6-030

The transverse-crib barn is not only widespread in the southern portions of the midwestern states where set-tlers from Kentucky constituted a large portion of the population; it is the dominant barn throughout the region. The great flexibility of the barn's design accounts for this widespread popularity; it could be used on farms devoted to livestock, dairy, poultry, grain, or corn. The barn provides a large storage area as well as an efficient-ly organized stable. Further, the barn could be easily expanded to accommodate increased production. Agricultural scientists trying to invent a modern barn at the end of the nineteenth century did little more than modify the dimensions of the usual transverse-crib barn.

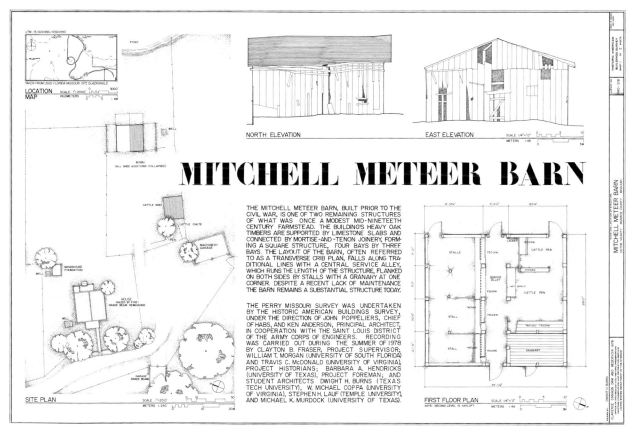

6-031. Mitchell Meteer Barn, Victor Vic., Monroe County, Missouri. Dwight H. Burns, delineator, 1978. P & P, HABS, MO-1218; HABS, MO, 64-6CT.V, 2- , sheet no. 1.

6-032. Reuben Ross Barn, Smithville Vic., Clay County, Missouri. Darl Rastorfer, delin-eator, 1978. P & P, HABS, MO-1223; HABS, MO, 24-SMITH.V, 1- , sheet no. 3.

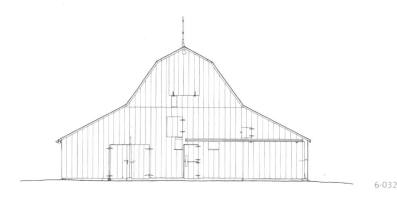

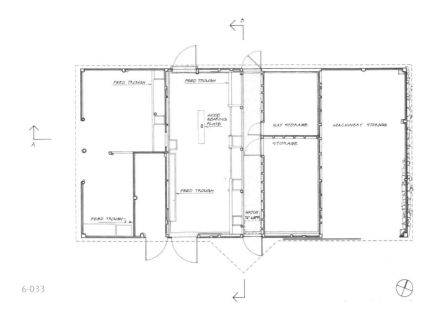

6-033

6-033. Reuben Ross Barn, Smithville Vic., Clay County, Missouri. Darl Rastorfer, delineator, 1978. P & P, HABS, MO-1223; HABS, MO, 24-SMITH.V, 1- , sheet no. 2.

6-034. Barn in central Ohio. Summer, 1938. Ben Shahn, photographer. P & P, LC-USF 33-006647-M3.

6-035. Barn near Marseilles, Illinois. January, 1937. Russell Lee, photographer. P & P, LC-USF 341-T-010196-B.

6-034

6-035

6-036. White Haven barn, Afton Vic., St. Louis County, Missouri.
Lester Jones, photographer, 1991. P & P, HABS, MO-1150-B;
HABS, MO, 95-AFT.V, 1C-1.

6-037. Turner barn, Glasgow Vic., Howard County, Missouri.
Charles van Ravenswaay, photographer, 1946. P & P, HABS,
MO-1483; HABS, MO, 45-GLASG.V, 3A-1.

6-038. Barn near Marseilles, Illinois. January, 1937.
Russell Lee, photographer. P & P, LC-USF 341-T-010198-B.

6-036

6-037

6-038

6-039

6-039. Barn near Hughesville, Missouri. November, 1939. Arthur Rothstein, photographer. P & P, LC-USF 34-29001-D.

6-040. Barn, Ray Conner Farm near Templeton, Indiana. March, 1937. Russell Lee, photographer. P & P, LC-USF 34-010571-D.

In this barn (and 6-041–6-052), the loft is increased by raising the height of the side walls. Barns with this taller profile constitute a subtype of the transverse-crib barn (compare 6-032–6-039).

6-040

6-041. Barn, Mary Lah Farm near Fowler, Indiana. February, 1937. Russell Lee, photographer. P & P, LC-USF 341-T-010486-B.

6-42. Barn, J. H. Herbrandson Farm near Estherville, Iowa. December, 1936. Russell Lee, photographer. P & P, LC-USF 34-010078-D.

6-043. Barn, Frank Chyle Farm, Protivin, Howard County, Iowa. Darrell Henning, photographer, 1988. P & P, HABS, IA-163-B; HABS, IOWA, 45-PROV, 1-B-1.

6-041

6-042

6-043

6-048

6-051

6-048. Barn, G. H. West Farm near Estherville, Iowa. December, 1936. Russell Lee, photographer. P & P, LC-USF 34-010076-D.

6-049. Barn, Veblen Farm, Nerstrand Vic., Rice County, Minnesota. Jet Lowe, photographer, 1987. P & P, HABS, MN-82-A; HABS, MINN, 66-NER.V, 1-A-5.

6-050. Barn near Little Fork, Minnesota. September, 1937. Russell Lee, photographer. P & P, LC-USF 342-T-030631-A.

6-051. Barn, Ray Merriot Farm near Estherville, Iowa. December, 1936. Russell Lee, photographer. P & P, LC-USF 34-010077-D.

6-049

6-050

6-052

6-052. Barn in Lake of the Woods County,
Minnesota. September, 1939. John Vachon,
photographer. P & P, LC-USF 33-1501-M2.

6-053. Barn, August Grettencord farm near
Fowler, Indiana. February, 1937. P & P,
LC-USF 341-T-010490-B.

Here a tall transverse-crib barn was expanded
by the addition of two flanking sheds that provided additional stabling and storage areas.
Later designers would prefer to increase the
capacity of a barn by adding to its length (see
6-057–6-061). Also note the large corncrib
next to the barn; it too follows the lines of a
transverse-crib barn. On a smaller farm, a
building of its dimensions easily would have
served as a barn.

6-053

6-054

6-055. John French barn, Deepwater Vic., Henry County, Missouri. Paul Piaget, photographer, 1977. P & P, HABS, MO-1245-A; HABS, MO, 42-DEEP.V, 5A-1.

Divided by a cross passage halfway along the central runway (see the plan, 6-056), this large barn was, in form, composed of two standard length transverse-crib barns, which commonly contained six cribs. The apparent design strategy used here reveals the persistence and the utility of the older traditional form.

6-054. Barn, William Keefe farm near Boswell, Indiana. February, 1937. Russell Lee, photographer. P & P, LC-USF 341-T-010503-B.

6-056. Floor plan, John French barn, Deepwater Vic., Henry County, Missouri. Gary D. Daker, delineator, 1977. P & P, HABS, MO-1245-A; HABS, MO, 42-DEEP.V, 5A- , sheet no. 1.

6-055

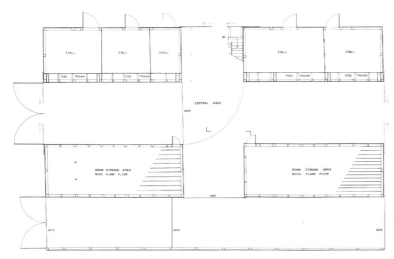

6-056

6-057. Dairy barn at Wabash Farms, Indiana. May, 1940. John Vachon, photographer. P & P, LC-USF 34-060947-D.

This barn (and those shown in 6-058–6-061) show the influence of barn designs generated by commercial designers like William Radford, whose book *Practical Barn Plans* (1908) offered plans for dairy barns that were both long and thin.

6-058. Dairy barn near Manitowoc, Wisconsin. June, 1945. Gottscho-Schleisner, Inc., photographers. P & P, Gottscho-Schleisner Collection, LC-G612-T-47439.

6-059. Dairy barn near Marion, Iowa. August, 1941. Marion Post Wolcott, photographer. P & P, LC-USF 34-90035-D.

6-057

6-058

6-059

6-060

6-060. Dairy barn in Dakota County, Minnesota. September, 1939. Arthur Rothstein, photographer. P & P, LC-USF 34-28122-D.

6-061. North dairy barn, Longview Farm, Lees Summit, Jackson County, Missouri. David J. Kaminsky, photographer, 1978. P & P, HABS, MO-1233; HABS, MO, 48-LESUM, 1/21-1.

6-061

FRENCH BARNS

The standard French barn or grange was similar to the English three-bay barn, consisting of a central threshing floor flanked by stables or storage areas. The Chevaux barn (6-062) was built of stone masonry but, over time, the structure was enveloped by framed wooden additions. The Valle barn (6-063 and 6-064) was essentially a horse stable built at the rear of a house lot. It provided a space where a wagon could be stored, along with two stables for horses and a loft area for storing hay.

6-062

6-063

6-062. Chevaux Barn, Perryville Vic., Perry County, Missouri, 1890. Alexander Piaget and Charles van Ravenswaay, photographers, 1937. P & P, HABS, MO-1560B; HABS, MO, 79-PER6.V, 1B-1.

6-063. Jean Baptiste Valle barn, St. Genevieve, St. Genevieve County, Missouri. Alexander Piaget and Charles van Ravenswaay, photographers, 1938–41. P & P, HABS, MO-31-10; HABS, MO, 97-SAIGEN, 1A-2.

6-064. Site plan, Jean Baptiste Valle house lot, St. Genevieve, St. Genevieve County, Missouri. T. A. Gruenhagen, delineator, 1985. P & P, HABS, MO-31-10; HABS, MO, 97-SAIGEN, 1-, sheet no. 2.

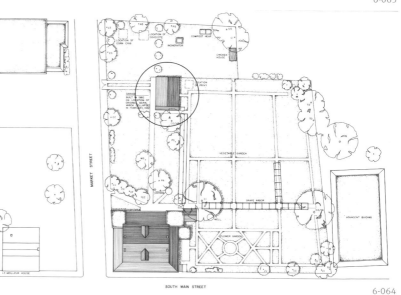

6-064

GERMAN BARNS

Large German communities formed during the 1830s along the Missouri River to the west of St. Louis and in Perry County on the Mississippi. Their barns ranged in type from archaic medieval style house-barns (6-079) to the sorts of bank barns built by an earlier generation of Germans who settled in Pennsylvania (6-070–6-075).

During the middle decades of the nineteenth century, Wisconsin welcomed German settlers both from Europe and Pennsylvania. Collectively they built both old-fashioned buildings (6-076, 6-077, 6-080) and more modern structures modified by as much as a century and a half of American experiences.

6-065

6-066

6-065. L. Schramm barn, Herman Vic., Gasconade County, Missouri. Alexander Piaget and Charles van Ravenswaay, photographers, 1938. P & P, HABS, MO-1433; HABS, MO, 37-HERM.V, 8A-1.

The Schramm barn (and 6-066–6-069) are examples of *Grundscheier* or ground barns. They are the formal equivalent of the English three-bay barn or the French grange.

6-066. Fuchs mill, Femme Osage Vic., St. Charles County, Missouri, ca. 1850. Paul Piaget, photographer, 1962. P & P, HABS, MO-1589; HABS, MO, 92-FEMO.V, 2A-1.

This building, constructed to house an ox-powered gristmill, was later transformed into a barn.

6-067. Freese barn, St. Charles, St. Charles County, Missouri, 1842. Paul Piaget, photographer, 1962. P & P, HABS, MO-1776-B; HABS, MO, 92-SAICH, 15B-1.

The walls of the Freese barn were constructed with a heavy timber frame in-filled with bricks known as half-timbering (called *fachwerk* in German).

6-068. Kramer-Witte barn, Owensville Vic., Gasconade County, Missouri, ca. 1860. Jet Lowe, photographer, 1983. P & P, HABS, MO-259; HABS, MO,37-OW6.V, 1A-5.

The Germanic identity of the Kramer-Witte barn is clearly evident since the distinctive half-timbered walls were left unsided.

6-067

6-068

6-074. Bank barn, Gingerich Farm, Versailles Vic., Morgan County, Missouri, ca. 1870. Alexander Piaget and Charles van Ravenswaay, photographers, 1939–41. P & P, HABS, MO-1546; HABS, MO, 71-VERS.V, 3-1.

This barn is an example of the English bank barn which used a pent roof to shelter the stable entrances in place of a forebay. That Morgan County was a conservative community is indicated by the fact that 6 percent of its residents continued to use German as a first language as late as 1974. Given the strength of ethnic identity in this county, this building most likely grew out of modest experimentation with a traditional plan rather than the wholesale borrowing of a new barn type.

6-075. Bank barn, Versailles Vic., Morgan County, Missouri, 1920. Alexander Piaget and Charles van Ravenswaay, photographers, 1941. P & P, HABS, MO-1547; HABS, MO, 71-VERS.V, 1-2.

6-076. Clarence Christian barn, Watertown Vic., Dodge County, Wisconsin. Cervin Robinson, photographer, 1960. P & P, HABS, WIS-148; HABS, WIS, 14-WATO.V, 1-3.

The presence of a forebay on a small building underscores the importance of the forebay among German farmers. For them it was a necessary element. The extra effort required to construct a forebay was considered a normative practice.

6-075

6-076

6-077. Kuenzi barn, Watertown Vic., Dodge County, Wisconsin. Cervin Robinson, photographer, 1960. P & P, HABS, WIS-151; HABS, WIS, 14-WATO.V, 3-1.

The Kuenzi barn offers a strong parallel to Missouri's German barns constructed with the *fachwerk* technique (compare with 6-068). The area around Watertown, Wisconsin, retains many German buildings that are more than 150 years old (see also 6-076, 6-080, and 6-081).

6-078. Floor plan, Kuenzi barn, Watertown Vic., Dodge County, Wisconsin. John S. Reynolds, F. Kempton Mooney, delineators, 1960. P & P, HABS, WIS-151; HABS, WIS, 14-WATO.V, 3-, sheet no. 2.

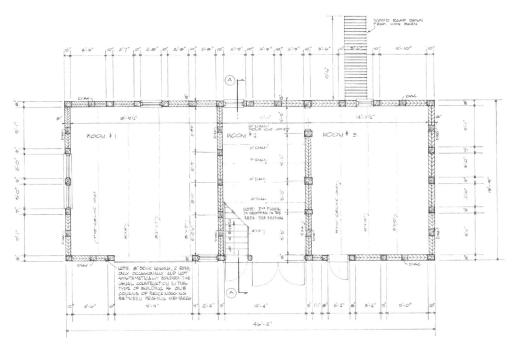

FLOOR PLAN
SCALE ¼" = 1'-0"

6-101. Corncrib, Plager Farm, Grundy County, Iowa. September, 1939. Arthur Rothstein, photographer. P & P, LC-USF 34-028204-D.

6-102. Corncrib in Boone County, Missouri. November, 1939. Arthur Rothstein, photographer. P & P, LC-USF 34-29124-D.

6-103. Corncrib near Fowler, Indiana. February, 1937. Russell Lee, photographer. P & P, LC-USF 341-10491-B.

6-079

6-079. Pelster house-barn, Detmold Vic., Franklin County, Missouri, ca. 1860. Jet Lowe, photographer, 1983. P & P, HABS, MO-244; HABS, MO 36-DET.V, 1-6.

The sheltering of humans and animals in a single building is a practice that extends back several millennia in Europe and one that is still practiced widely in Germany and Switzerland. The combining of house and barn functions under a single roof was generally abandoned when European settlers arrived on American shores, although it is hinted at in the linear arrangement of some Mid-Atlantic farms (see 3-064). But in the newly formed German enclaves on the distant western frontier during the first half of the nineteenth century a retreat to old ways seemed most prudent. Thus it was that Friedrich Wilhelm Pelster was moved to build an *Einhaus*, a house-barn, on his newly purchased 40-acre parcel of land located about 50 miles west of St. Louis.

6-098

6-099

6-100

This modest cattle ranch was located in the high plains of the Texas panhandle. Note the long cattle shed in the foreground with a tall stack of fodder off to one side. The wind-driven pump draws a supply of water up from the high plains aquifer to fill the tank standing in the background. The homestead is at right.

7-001

7-002

7-003. Spanish-American farm and orchard near Mora, New Mexico. September, 1939. Russell Lee, photographer. P & P, LC-USF 34-034309-D.

7-004. Farm near Chamizal, New Mexico. July, 1940. Russell Lee, photographer. P & P, LC-USF 34-37100-D.

7-005. The Mutz ranch, Colfax County, New Mexico. 1943. John Collier, photographer. P & P, LC-USF 3-18618-C.

7-003

7-004

7-005

7-006

7-006. Farm near Llano de San Juan, New Mexico. August, 1940. Russell Lee, photographer. P & P, LC-USF 34-37208-D.

7-007. Cattle ranch near Springerville, Arizona. April,1940. Russell Lee, photographer. P & P, LC-USF 34-035877-D.

7-007

SOUTHERN BARN TYPES

Because much of the eastern half of Texas lies within the coastal plain of the Gulf Coast, it should be seen as the westernmost portion of the lowland South. The presence of southern barn types in this area proves that cultural migrations do not pay heed to state boundaries. Varieties of the single-pen and transverse-crib barn are commonplace in this part of the state.

7-008

7-008. Single-crib log barn near Marshall, Texas, ca. 1939. Photographer unknown. P & P, LC-USF 33-012184-M1.

Compare with 6-009–6-012.

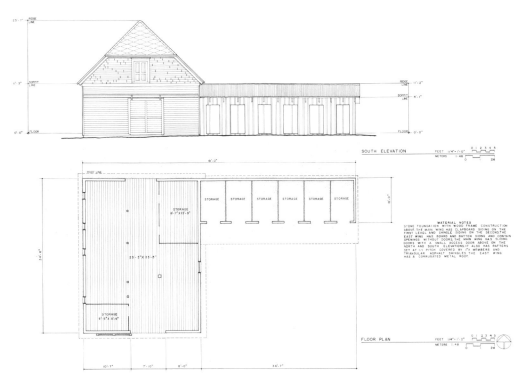

7-012

7-013. South elevation and floor plan, first barn, Mabel Doss Day Lea House, Voss Vic., Coleman County, Texas. Robert Holton, Chris Lammers, Brian Dougan, delineators, 1989. P & P, HABS, TX-3351-F; HABS, TEX, 42-VOS.V, 8F- , sheet no. 1.

Mabel Doss Day Lea was, during the early decades of the twentieth century, known as the "Cattle Queen of Texas." Her ranch in Coleman County comprised some 80,000 acres of range land. This barn was used to store hay; a line of horse stalls was appended to the east side of the barn. While designed to shelter horses, these stalls were actually used as granaries.

7-013. Barn, Travis County, Texas. March, 1940. Russell Lee, photographer. P & P, LC-USF 34-035743-D.

This substantial barn stood on a portion of the richest farmland in Texas, known as the Black Waxy Prairie. A barn with these proportions would have fit easily into the farming landscapes of the Midwest (compare with 6-039 and 6-042).

7-013